Hydraulics and Electro-hydraulics

Volume 1: Hydraulic Pumps and the Power Pack on Ships

To
The Next Generation of Seafarers

Hydraulics and Electro-hydraulics

Volume 1: Hydraulic Pumps and the Power Pack on Ships

J. Majumder

Elstan A. Fernandez

SHROFF PUBLISHERS & DISTRIBUTORS PVT. LTD.
Mumbai   Bangalore   Kolkata   New Delhi

Hydraulics and Electro-hydraulics
Volume 1: Hydraulic Pumps and the Power Pack on Ships

By *J. Majumder, Elstan A. Fernandez*

Copyright © 2022 – *J. Majumder, Elstan A. Fernandez*

First Edition: November 2022

Print ISBN: 978-93-5542-301-6

E_Book ISBN: 978-93-5542-318-4

Published by **Shroff Publishers and Distributors Pvt. Ltd.** B-103, Railway Commercial Complex, Sector 3, Sanpada (E), Navi Mumbai 400705 TEL: (91 22) 4158 4158 • FAX: (91 22) 4158 4141 E-mail : spdorders@shroffpublishers.com • Web : www.shroffpublishers.com Printed at SAP Print Solutions Pvt. Ltd., Mumbai

Preface to the First Edition

This pocket book is based on an extract from the book titled Hydraulics for Mariners. It deals with understanding of the fundamentals of hydraulics, various pumps, and the hydraulic power pack.

The Pocket Book Series was introduced because there is a changing trend in the way books are read today. The new normal is that readers and students prefer to read specific, and not so voluminous content, in the least time, as time comes at a premium these days.

Hopefully our team of authors will be able to cater to numerous topics from many relevant subjects.

Any feedback is always welcome!

J. Majumder & Elstan A. Fernandez

Acknowledgement

The opportunity to share our acquired knowledge with thousands of professionals and students across many countries and organisations has given me an immense sense of accomplishment and satisfaction. It has also been a wonderful journey of discovery for me - both while researching for this book and teaching the subject in India and abroad.

This book is the result of over 40 years of learning and hands-on experience in this field, including over 20 years of research and collaboration with various organisations and specialists in the global maritime industry.

We sincerely thank all the wonderful people who have supported me in every way, ever since We embarked on this project.

We am indebted to many distinguished persons who have have not only supported our endeavours but also permitted me to publish very valuable content for education. These articles are relevant to the building, safe operation and conscientious survey of commercial ships. Many world-class organisations and manufacturers have extended their invaluable support too. We are grateful for the updated information from their websites and related literature. These inclusions have undoubtedly enriched the content.

Numerous students now realize their dream of being educated through a scholarship program that is funded by the royalty that we receive.

The encouragement from lay people and professionals alike has thus been a stimulus to our enthusiasm. In order to give back and say "thank you" to the maritime fraternity, we also host a free educational website – www.marineelectricity.com.

In this context, we have a beautiful quote to share with our readers:

"Real knowledge, like everything else of value, is not to be obtained easily.

It must be worked for, studied for, thought for, and, more than all must be prayed for."

Thomas Arnold (1795-1842), British Educator, Scholar

Contents

Contents

Chapter 1
Introduction to Hydraulics

1.1 Fluid Power

Fluid power is known to have the highest power density of all conventional power-transmission technologies. "Fluid Power" is a term which was created to include the generation, control and application of smooth, effective power of compressed fluids - either liquids or gases when this power is used to provide force and motion to mechanisms.

This force and motion maybe in the form of pushing, pulling, rotating, regulating or driving. Fluid power includes hydraulics, which involves liquids and pneumatics, which involves gases.

1.2 Definition of Hydraulics

Old Definition: Anything which is in affiliation with water is called hydraulics.

New Era Definition: The transmission and control of forces and movements by means of fluids is called hydraulics. The word "hydraulics" is derived from a Greek word "hydraulikos" which in turn originates from (*hydor* for water and *aulos* for pipe in Greek). Hydraulics is the science of transmitting force or motion through the medium of a confined liquid to perform mechanical tasks.

Liquid is almost incompressible, meaning that a liquid's particles are very close together. When the particles move, they strike each other and also bump against the walls of the container. The pressure in a liquid transfer being in equal measure in every direction, a force applied at one point on a liquid, is transferred to other points on the liquid.

1.3   The Inception of Power Transmission by Fluid

Power transmission by fluid power was put into engineering practice more than hundred years after French physicist Pascal, by the Englishman Bramah who showed the world in his own hydraulic press, how, out of a relatively small effort on a long stroke, small diameter piston a very large force on a short stroke large diameter piston could be produced.

1.4   Fluid Power Principles

1.4.1   Pascal's Law

Fluid or Hydraulic power transmission is based on the principle of a French Physicist, Pascal in 1648 which states that:

(1) Pressure works on a plane at a right angle.

(2) Pressure is transmitted equally in all directions.

(3) Pressure applied on part of a fluid is transmitted throughout the fluid equally.

Pressurized liquids can be mode of power transmission over medium distances by first converting mechanical power into hydraulic power and then finally reconverting hydraulic power back into mechanical power.

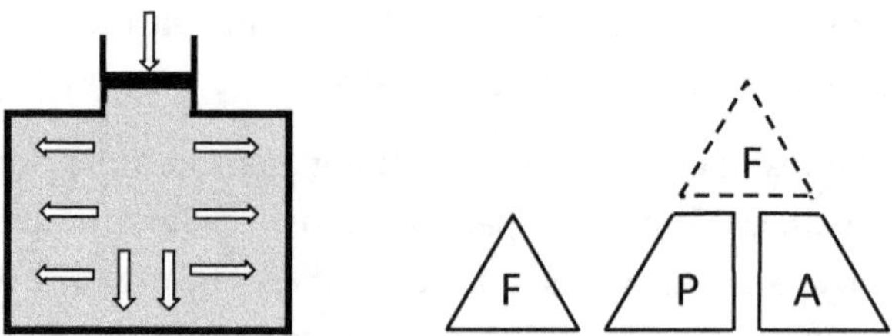

Figure 1.1 – Relationship between Force, Pressure and Area

The applied force is given by the expression F = (P x A)

P is the pressure in Pascals, F is the force in Newtons and A is the cross-sectional area in m^2. Essentially, if two cylinders are connected - a large one and a small one and when a force is applied to one cylinder, it generates equal pressure in both cylinders. As one cylinder contains a larger volume, the force that the larger cylinder produces is higher, although the pressure in the two cylinders remains the same. Since the pressure is transmitted equally throughout the fluid in all directions according to Pascal's Principle, P_1 must equal P_2.

$$P_1 = P_2 \rightarrow \frac{F_1}{A_1} = \frac{F_2}{A_2} \qquad\qquad F_2 = \left(\frac{A_2}{A_1}\right)F_1$$

Rearranging to solve for F_2, you find that F_2 is increased by the ratio of the areas A_2 over A_1. As shown in the Figure 1.2 force F_2 is 20 times more than force F_1.

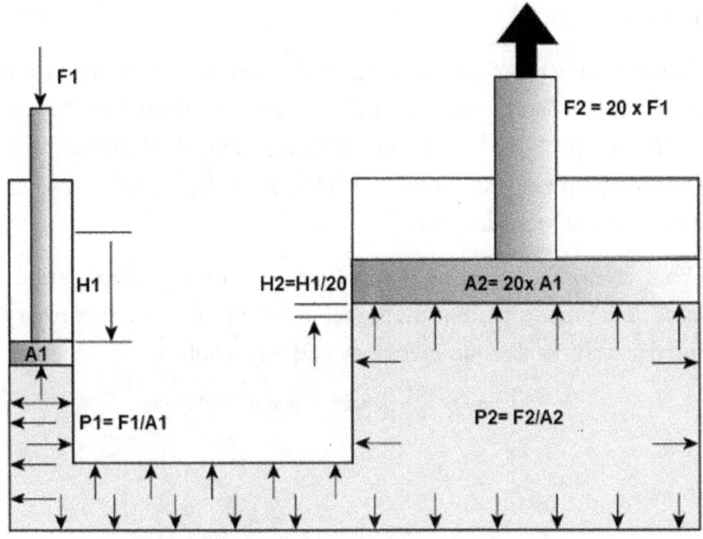

Figure 1.2 – Application of Pascal's Law

Since energy or power is always conserved, the amplification in force must result in a reduction of the fluid velocity. Indeed, if the resultant force is applied over a larger area then a unit displacement of the area would cause a larger volumetric displacement than a unit displacement of the small area through which the generating force is applied.

So, we can conclude that in hydraulic systems, a small force across a small cross-sectional area transmits pressure and creates a large force over a larger cross-sectional area which thus creates a mechanical advantage.

Thus, what is gained in force must be sacrificed in distance or speed and power would be conserved. As shown in Figure 1.2,

$$F_1 \times H_1 = F_2 \times H_2 \quad So \ H_1 = F_2 / F_1 * H_2 = A_2/A_1 * H_2 \quad or \quad H_2 = 20 / H_1$$

The displacement H_2 of a big piston is 20 x less than the small piston's displacement H_1.

If a hydraulic rotary pump with the flow 20 cc / revolution is connected to a hydraulic rotary motor with 200 cc/rev, the shaft torque required to drive the pump is $1/10^{th}$ of the torque than that available at the motor shaft, but the shaft speed (revolutions / minute) for the motor is also only one tenth of the pump's shaft speed.

This combination is the same type of force multiplication as the cylinder example, just that the linear force in this case is a rotary force, defined as torque. Torque increases with Hydraulics.

$$T_{motor} = (V_{motor} / V_{pump}) \times T_{pump}$$

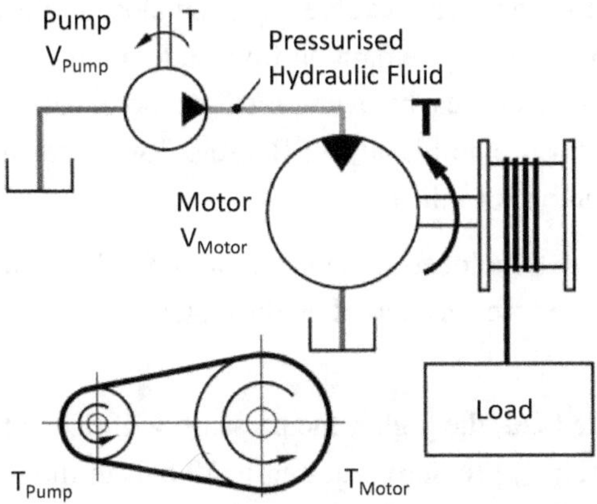

Figure 1.3 – Mechanical analogy of a Hydraulic System

The example shown in Figure 1.3 is usually referred to as a hydraulic transmission involving a certain hydraulic "gear ratio".

1.4.2 Pressure

Pressure along with flow is one of the key parameters involved in the study of hydraulics. It is a popular misconception that the hydraulic pump creates pressure in a hydraulic system. The fact is that pumps create flow, not pressure. Pressure is the resistance to flow and the load determines it. All points of resistance in series contribute to the total system pressure.

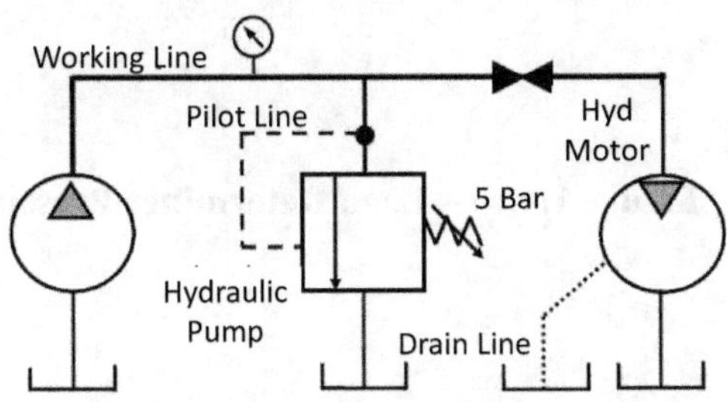

Figure 1.4(a) - Pressure Resistance to Flow

In Figure 1.4, the manual valve has been closed, blocking the flow to the load motor. The only remaining flow path is through the relief valve. A resistance of 5 Bar must be overcome for fluid to pass through the relief valve. Once pressure builds up to 5 Bar, the flow is delivered through the relief valve and back to the tank.

The pressure developed in an actuator depends on the load. Pressure will rise until the force is exerted on the piston in a cylinder can move the load.

The greater the load, the higher the pressure will rise, which can be seen from Figure 1.4(b), pressure required is 30 bar, to move the load that is increased from 500 kgs to 1500 kgs.

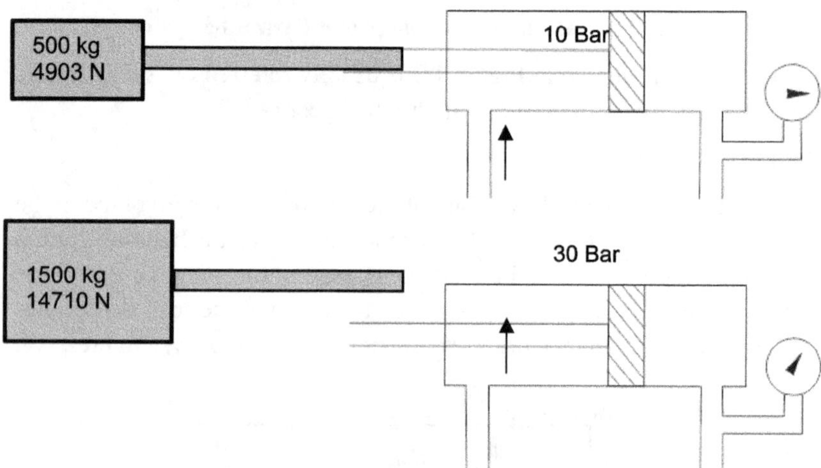

Figure 1.4(a) – Load Determines Pressure

1.4.2.1   *Hydraulic Pressure in a Parallel Circuit*

In a hydraulic system with parallel circuits, the pump's oil follows through the path of least resistance. The pump supplies oil to three parallel circuits as shown in the Figure 1.4**(c)**. Circuit 3 has the lowest resistance and therefore would have the highest priority and Circuit 1 has the highest resistance and therefore would have the lowest priority. When the pump's oil flow fills the passage from the pump to the valves, the pump's oil pressure increases to 10 Bar, created by the restriction of oil flow, opens the valve to Circuit 3 and oil flows into the circuit. When Circuit 3 fills, the fluid pressure will increase to 30 bar and opens the valve in Circuit 2. Similarly, circuit pressure will increase to 60 Bar due to Circuit 1's restriction.

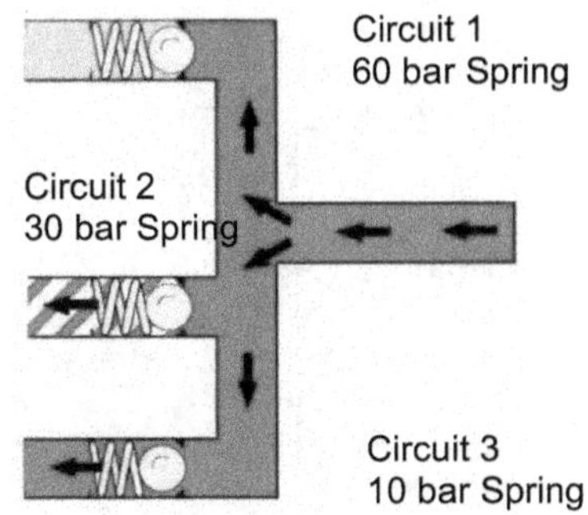

Figure 1.4(c)
Parallel Resistance and Pressure

1.4.2.2 Hydraulic Pressure in Series Circuit

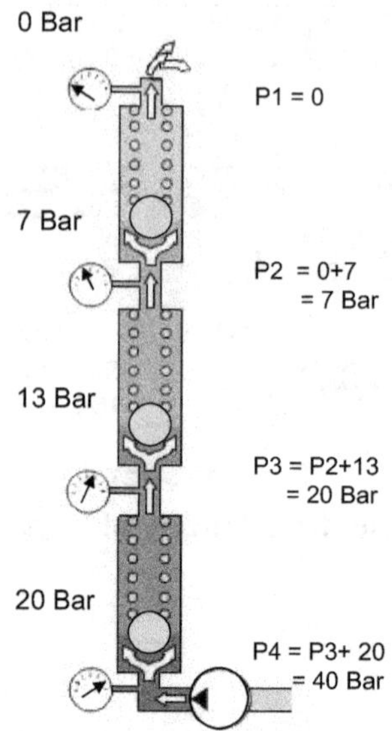

Figure 1.5 – Series Resistance and Pressure

If we consider a hydraulic pump without restrictions, it produces only flow and not pressure. However, any restriction in the flow from the pump results in the formation of pressure which can be seen from Figure 1.5. The hydraulic pump delivers the fluid at a pressure of 40 Bar due to the added series resistance. Restriction or resistance to flow normally results from the load induced in the actuator. The various conductors and components of a hydraulic system such as pipes and elbows also act as points of resistance and contribute to the generation of pressure in the system. The pressure in a static fluid must have the following properties:

a) The pressure works perpendicular to the surface of the plane.
b) The pressure at each point is the same for   all directions.

1 Pascal	1 N/m^2
105 Pa	0.1 MPa
1 bar	100,000 Pa
1 bar	14.5 psi

Table 1.1 – Pressure Units

1.4.3 Flow of Fluid (Movement Depends on Flow)

Flow is the action in the hydraulic system that gives the actuator its motion. Nothing moves without flow. Pressure gives the actuator its force, but flow is essential to cause movement. Flow in the hydraulic system is created by the pump. Flow rate is a measure of the volume of fluid passing a point in a given time. Pressure indicates work load. The flow of fluid in a hydraulic system is also the means used for transferring the applied pressure through the system to cause work to be conducted, which makes the actuator operation possible.

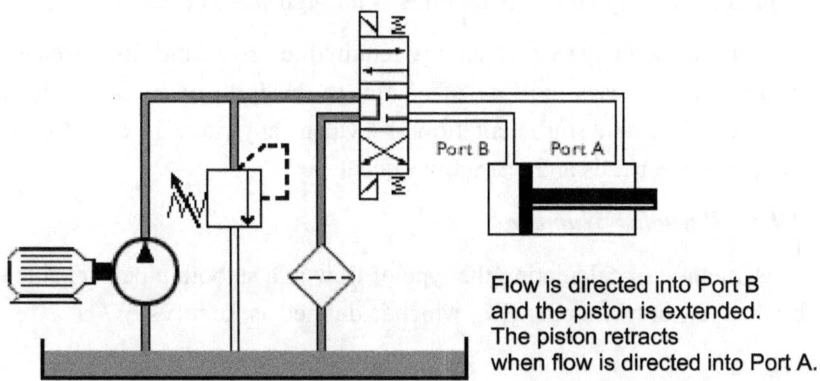

Figure 1.6 - Flow in Fluid Causes Motion in Actuator

1.4.4 Types of Fluid Flow

When the system is properly designed, the flow of a fluid results in laminar flow, when each particle of the fluid follows a smooth path i.e., paths which never interfere with one another and that the velocity of the fluid is constant at any point in the fluid.

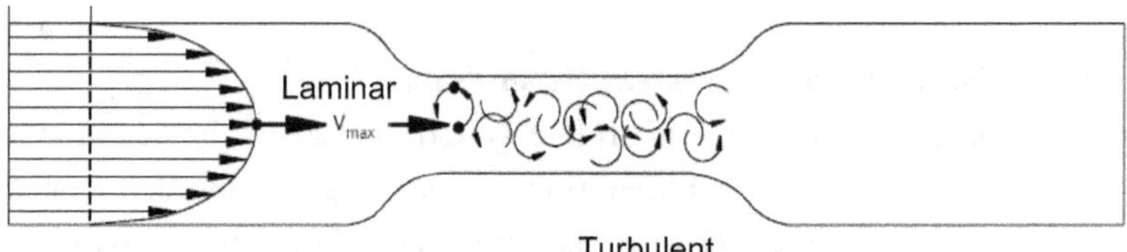

Figure 1.7 - Laminar and Turbulent Flow in Fluid

The fluid flow in which the adjacent layers of the fluid cross each other and do not move parallel to each other, is called turbulent flow.

Turbulent flow occurs in large diameter pipes in which fluid flows with high velocity and kinked lines or through sharp bends.

Turbulence increases the energy required to drive fluid flow because turbulence increases the loss of energy in the form of friction, which generates heat and turbulent flow is evident anywhere in a hydraulic system where bends and restrictions occur.

1.4.5 Reynolds' Number

A method of calculating the type of flow in a smooth pipe is enabled by the Reynolds' number (Re) which is defined as Re = (v . d) / v.

Where:

- Flow velocity of the liquid is v (m/s)

- Pipe diameter is d (m)

- Kinetic viscosity is v (m^2/s)

A Reynolds' number of 2000 is the decisive value for marking a borderline between laminar flow and turbulent flow.

Experiments have demonstrated that for a Reynolds number below 2000, the flow is found to be laminar and above 4000, the flow is found to be turbulent.

The Reynolds number regime between 2000 and 4000 can be considered as the critical zone. The value 2300 is termed the critical Reynolds' number (R_{ecrit}) for smooth round pipes. Turbulent flow does not immediately become laminar on falling below (R_{ecrit}).

1.4.6 Flow Components

Flow has two components to consider flow velocity and flow rate.

1.4.7 Flow Velocity

It is the average speed of the fluid's particles past a given point or the average distance the particles travel per unit of time. The unit is meters / second or meters / minute. As the flow velocity increases, heat also increases due to friction which is caused by the fluid molecules rubbing against the inside surface of hoses and pipes.

1.4.8 Flow Rate

It is the volume of fluid passing a point in a given time designated as Q.

The following equation applies:

$Q = V/t$; Q = Flow rate (m^3/s), V = Volume (m^3), t = time (sec).

So, flow rate $V = Q \times t$. The unit is cm^3 / min or litres / min (cubic centimetres / minute or litres / min).

1.4.9   Relationship between Flow Rate and Velocity

The flow rate through a pipe is equal to the product of the flow velocity through a pipe and cross-sectional area of the pipe. The following example illustrates this relationship:

Example:

Oil flows through a hydraulic pipe of 30 mm diameter at a flow rate of 20 litres per minute. Find the flow velocity:

Solution:

$$\text{Flowrate, } V = \frac{\text{Flow rate, Q}}{\text{Cross-sectional area of the pipe, A}}$$

$$\text{Given } Q = 20 \text{ litres per min} = \frac{20 \times 1000}{60} = 333.3 \text{ m/sec}$$

$$\text{And } A = \frac{\Pi}{4} \times \left(\frac{30}{10}\right)^2 = 0.785 \times 9 = 7.065 \text{ cm}^2$$

$$\therefore V = \frac{Q}{A} = \frac{333.3}{7.065} = 47.18 \text{ cm}^2/\text{sec} = 0.472 \text{ m}^2/\text{sec}$$

1.4.10   Flow / Speed Relationship (Rate of Flow Determines Speed)

The speed of an actuator depends on the actuator size and the rate of flow into it.

$$Q = A \times V$$

Q = Flow in cm^3 / min, A = Area in cm^2, V = Velocity in cm / min

Flow = Displacement x Speed or Speed = Flow / Displacement

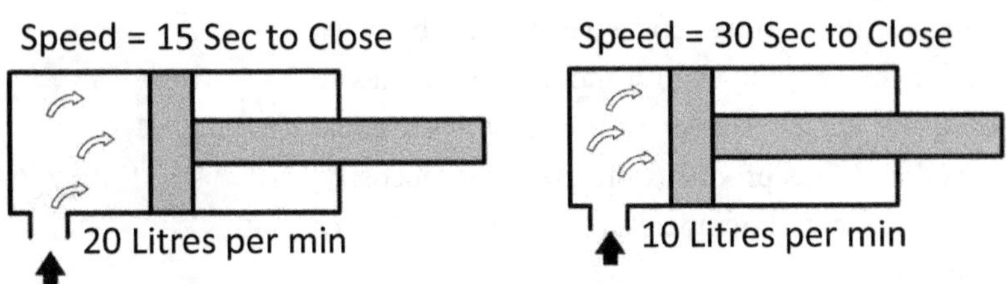

Figure 1.8 - Actuator Speed Control with Flow

With a given flow rate the actuator volume affects the actuator speed. Lesser the volume, faster is the speed of the actuator.

1.5   Viscosity

Viscosity is a measure of the resistance of a fluid which is being deformed by either shear stress or tensile stress.

At a molecular level, viscosity is a result of the interaction between the different molecules in a fluid which can be described as friction between the molecules in the fluid.

So, viscosity can be defined "thickness" or "internal friction" for fluids.

Thus, water is "thin", having a lower viscosity, while honey is "thick", having a higher viscosity. Put simply, the less viscous the fluid is, the greater its fluidity or ease of movement.

1.5.1   Causes of Viscosity

The causes of viscosity in a fluid are possibly attributed to two factors:

(i)   Intermolecular force of cohesion
(ii) Molecular momentum exchange

Due to the strong cohesive forces between molecules, any layer in a moving fluid tries to drag the adjacent layer to move with an equal speed and thus produces the effect of viscosity; it decreases with temperature as cohesive forces decrease.

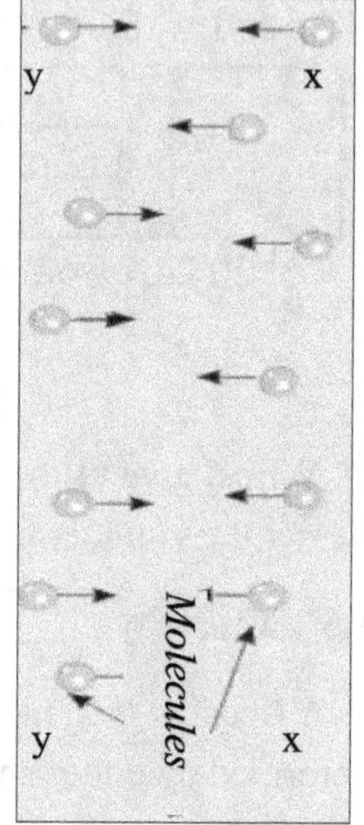

❖ The molecules from layer xx in course of continuous thermal agitation migrate into layer yy.

❖ The momentum from the migrant molecules from layer xx is stored by molecules of layer yy by way of collision. Thus, layer yy as a whole is sped up.

❖ The molecules from the lower layer yy arrive at xx and tend to retard the layer xx.

❖ Every such migration of molecules causes forces of acceleration or deceleration to drag the layers to oppose the differences in velocity between the layers and produce the effect of viscosity.

Figure 1.9 - Movement of Fluid Molecules
Between Two Adjacent Moving Layers

As the random molecular motion increases with a rise in temperature, the viscosity also increases accordingly. Except for very high pressure, the viscosity of both liquids and gases ceases to be a function of pressure.

For gases, molecular motion is more significant than the cohesive forces, thus viscosity of gases increase with increase in temperature.

For Newtonian fluids, the coefficient of viscosity depends strongly on temperature but varies very little with pressure.

1.5.2 Property of Viscosity

A high viscosity implies a high resistance to flow while a low viscosity indicates a low resistance to flow. Viscosity varies inversely with temperature. Viscosity is also affected by pressure; higher pressure causes the viscosity to increase and subsequently the load-carrying capacity of the oil also increases.

This property enables the use of thin oils to lubricate heavy machinery. The load-carrying capacity also increases as the operating speed of the lubricated machinery is increased. The two related measures of fluid viscosity are dynamic (or absolute) and kinematic.

1.5.3 Dynamic (Absolute) Viscosity

The coefficient of absolute viscosity is a measure of internal resistance. Dynamic (absolute) viscosity is the tangential force per unit area required to move one horizontal plane with respect to another plane at a unit velocity when maintaining a unit distance apart in the fluid.

The shearing stress between the layers of a non-turbulent fluid moving in straight parallel lines can be defined for a Newtonian fluid as:

$$\tau = \mu \, dc \, / \, dy$$

$$= \mu \, \gamma \, \dots \, (1)$$

Where:

τ = shearing stress in fluid (N/m^2)

μ = dynamic viscosity of fluid $(N \, s/m^2)$

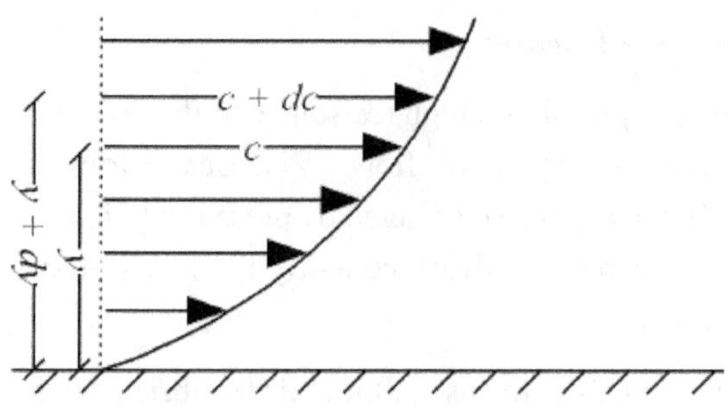

Figure 1.10 – Dynamic Viscosity

dc = unit velocity (m/s)

dy = unit distance between layers (m)

γ = dc / dy = shear rate (s-1)

Equation (1) is known as the Newtons Law of Friction which can be re-arranged to express dynamic viscosity as:

$\mu = \tau$ dy / dc

$\quad = \tau / \gamma$ ... (1b)

In the SI system, the dynamic viscosity units are N s/m^2, Pa s or kg/(m s) – where:

1 Pa s = 1 N s/m^2 = 1 kg/(ms)

1.5.4   Kinematic Viscosity

Kinematic viscosity is the ratio of - absolute (or dynamic) viscosity to density - a quantity in which no force is involved.

Kinematic viscosity can be obtained by dividing the absolute viscosity of a fluid with the fluid mass density like:

$\nu = \mu / \rho$...(2)

Where:

ν = kinematic viscosity (m^2/s)

μ = absolute or dynamic viscosity (N s/m^2)

ρ = density (kg/m^3)

In the SI-system the theoretical unit of kinematic viscosity is m^2/s - or the commonly used Stoke (St)

The physical variable "kinematic viscosity" is also referred to simply as "viscosity".

1.5.5   Compressibility and Bulk Modulus

Hydraulic fluids exhibit some degree of compressibility as a result of increase in pressure. The compressibility is the degree to which the fluid undergoes a reduction in volume under increased pressure.

Compressibility is the reciprocal of bulk modulus.

$B = -\Delta P / (\Delta V / V)$

B is the bulk modulus, in bar (or psi), ΔP is the differential pressure, in bar (or psi),

ΔV the differential volume change, in m^3 (or in^3),

V the original volume of the fluid, in m^3 (or in^3)

The bulk modulus of a newly purchased hydraulic fluid is typically about 17,000 bar, (or 246,564 psi).

Units of Kinematic Viscosity

- 1 stoke = 1 cm^2/s
- 1 cSt = 0.01 stoke
- 1 cSt = 1 mm^2/s

1.5.6 Effect of the Viscosity of a Fluid in Hydraulic System

Viscosity is the most important characteristic of a hydraulic fluid and has a significant impact on the operation of a hydraulic system. If the viscosity is too high then friction, pressure drop, power consumption and heat generation increase. Furthermore, sluggish operation of valves and servos may be the result.

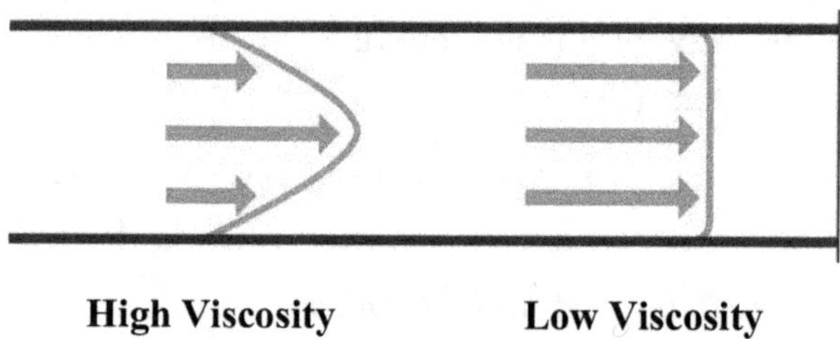

High Viscosity   **Low Viscosity**

If the viscosity is too low, increased internal and external leakage may result under higher operating temperatures. The oil film may be insufficient to prevent excessive wear or possible seizure of the moving parts, pump efficiency may decrease and sluggish operation due to lower pressure and loss of precise control may be experienced.

1.5.7 Friction, Heat and Pressure Drop

Friction occurs in all devices and lines in a hydraulic system through which liquid passes. This external friction is mainly at the line walls. There is also internal friction between the layers of liquid. The friction causes the hydraulic fluid and consequently also the components, to be heated. As a result of this heat generation, the pressure in the system drops and thus reduces the actual pressure at the drive section. The quantum of the pressure drop is based on the internal resistances in a hydraulic system. These are dependent on:

a) Flow velocity (cross-sectional area, flow rate).

b) Type of flow namely laminar or turbulent.

c) Type and number of cross-sectional reductions in the system of lines (throttles, orifices).

d) Viscosity of the oil (temperature, pressure).

e) Line length and flow diversion.

f) Surface finish.

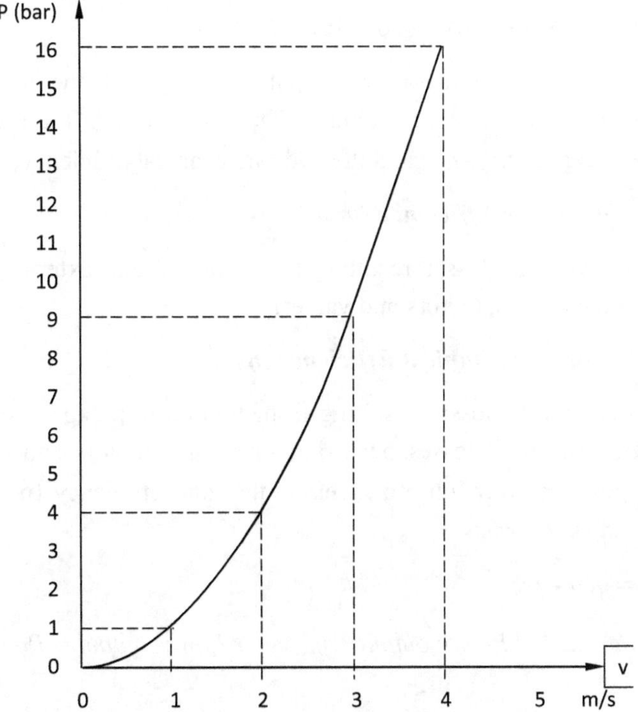

Figure 1.11 – Flow Rate and Pressure

The flow velocity has the greatest effect on the internal resistances since the resistance rises in proportion to the square of the velocity.

1.5.8 Hydraulic Power

Power in hydraulics is defined as flow multiplied by pressure. The hydraulic power supplied by a pump is:

Power = (P x Q) ÷ 600 where power is in kilowatts (kW), P is the pressure in bars, Q is the flow in litres per minute.

For example, if a pump delivers 200 litres / minute and the pressure is 300 bar, then the power of the pump is:

Power = (200 x 300) ÷ 600 = 100 kW.

When calculating the power input to the pump, the total pump efficiency η total must be included. This efficiency is the product of volumetric efficiency, η_{vol} and the hydromechanical efficiency, η_{hm}.

1.5.9 Volumetric Efficiency (η_{vol})

This covers the losses resulting from internal and external leakage losses in the pumps, motors and valves.

1.5.10 Hydro-mechanical Efficiency (η_{hm})

This covers the losses resulting from friction in pumps, motors and cylinders. The total losses occurring in pumps, motors and cylinders during power conversion are given as the total efficiency (η_{tot}) and is calculated as follows:

$$\eta_{tot} = \eta_{vol} \cdot \eta_{hm}$$

Power input = Power output ÷ η_{total} Or Power output = Power input x η_{total}

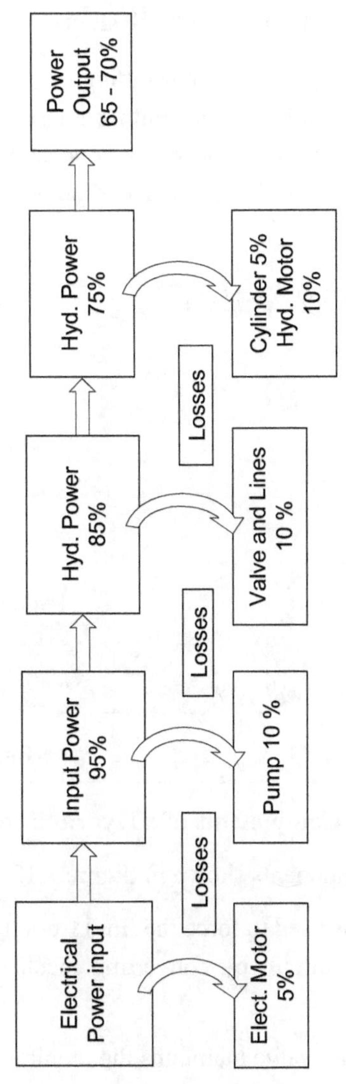

Figure 1.12 – Calculation of Input and Output Power in a Hydraulic System

1.6 Basic Components of a Hydraulic System

Hydraulic systems are power-transmitting assemblies employing pressurized liquid as a fluid for transmitting energy from an energy-generating source to an energy-using point to accomplish useful work. Figure 1.13 shows a simple circuit of a hydraulic system with basic components.

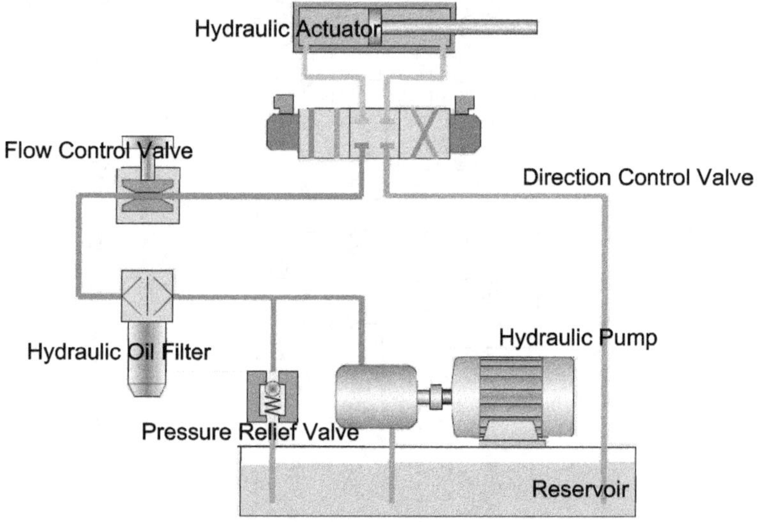

Figure 1.13 - Components of a Hydraulic System

The functions of the components shown in Figure 1.13 are as follows:

1) The hydraulic pump is used to force the fluid from the reservoir to the rest of the hydraulic circuit by converting mechanical energy into hydraulic energy.

2) The pressure regulating valve maintains the required level of pressure in the hydraulic fluid.

3) Filters are used to remove any foreign particles so as to keep the fluid system clean and efficient, as well as avoid damage to the actuators and valves.

4) Valves are used to control the direction, pressure and flow rate of a fluid flowing through the circuit.

5) A reservoir is used to hold the hydraulic liquid, usually hydraulic oil.

6) The piping system carries the hydraulic oil from one place to another.

7) The hydraulic actuator is a device used to convert the fluid power into mechanical power to do useful work. The actuator may be of the linear type (e.g., hydraulic cylinder) or rotary type (e.g., hydraulic motor) to provide linear or rotary motion, respectively.

There are two types of hydraulic systems used in fluid power applications which are described as Open Loop and Closed Loop systems.

1.7   Open Loop Circuits

The Hydraulic circuit shown in Figure 1.14 is of an open-loop type with fluid transferred from the storage tank to one side of the piston and returned from the other side of the piston to the tank.

Fluid is drawn from the tank by a pump that produces fluid flow at the required level of pressure. If the fluid pressure exceeds the required level, then the excess fluid returns to the reservoir and remains there until the pressure acquires the required level. These are circuits where both the inlet to the hydraulic pump and return from the motor or cylinder / piston are connected to a hydraulic reservoir. The hydraulic flow from the pressure port on the pump is directed to the device that it is powering and then returned to the reservoir. A relief valve or directional valve in the circuit may divert any unused fluid back to the reservoir.

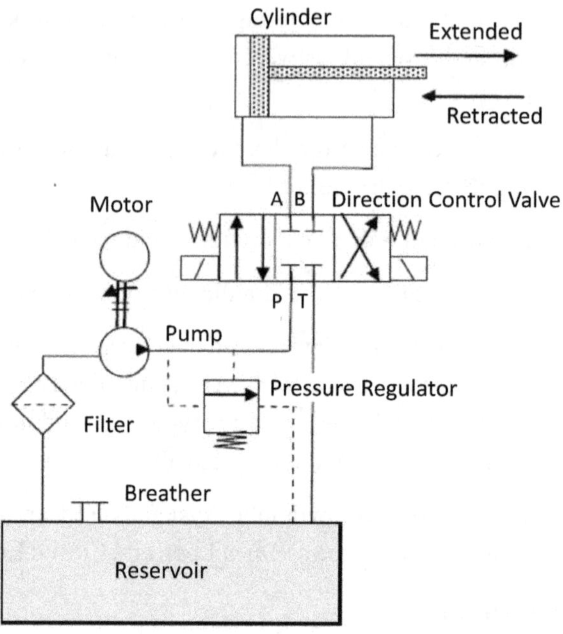

Figure 1.14 - Components of an Open loop Hydraulic System

Suction strainers and return filters keep the fluid clean. Cylinder movement is controlled by a three-position directional control valve.

1. When the piston of the valve is changed to the upper position, the pipe pressure line is connected to port A and thus the load is extended.

2. When the position of the valve is changed to the lower position, the pipe pressure line is connected to port B and thus the load is retracted.

3. When the valve is at the centre position, it locks the fluid into the cylinder thereby holding it in position and dead ends the fluid line causing all the pump output fluid to return to the tank via the pressure relief valve.

The advantages of an open loop system are:

- Generally, it is less expensive.

- It is better for lower pressure applications (below 3000 psi).

- It is simple to maintain and easier to diagnose problems if they occur.

The disadvantages of an open loop are:

- It could create heat in the system if the working pressure exceeds the relief valve setting when using fixed displacement pumps.

- The reservoir size must be larger for adequate cooling of the fluid.

1.8   Closed Loop Circuits

In case of a closed loop hydraulic system, the fluid will flow from the pump to the actuators i.e., the hydraulic motor and actuators to the pump continuously as shown in Figure 1.15.

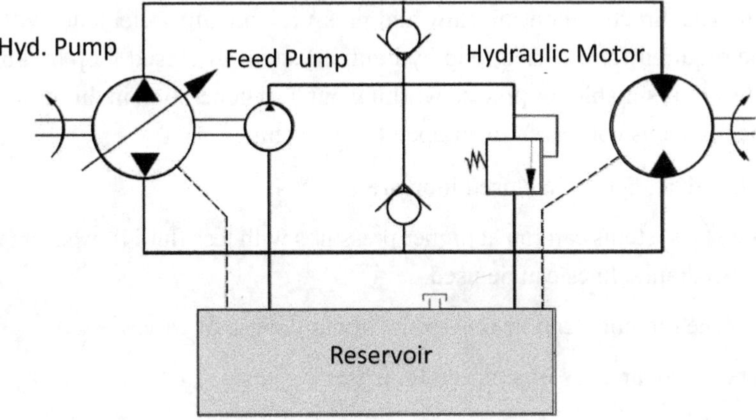

Figure 1.15 - Components of A Closed Loop Hydraulic System

Hydraulic fluid will enter at the inlet of the pump after passing through the actuators. One hydraulic pump might be used for driving multiple hydraulic motors in case of a closed loop hydraulic system.

The hydraulic pump will deliver the fluid to the actuators and will receive the same quantity of fluid from its inlet port from the actuators for smooth operation of the system. However, one feed pump is always provided with a closed loop hydraulic system in order to make-up the fluid in a closed loop circuit. The feed pump will be a fixed displacement one with a capacity approximately 15% of the main pump.'

In case of a closed loop hydraulic system, the main hydraulic pump can deliver the high-pressure fluid from both of its ports and therefore the main pump will control the direction of rotation of the hydraulic motor i.e., the main pump can control the direction of rotation of the hydraulic motor. The main pump can also control the pressure and flow of the fluid in a closed loop hydraulic system and that's why controlling elements such as direction control, flow and pressure regulating elements will not be required for a closed loop hydraulic system. A closed loop hydraulic system is suitable for precise working but heat generation in this case will be higher as compared to an open loop system.

The advantages of a closed loop are:

- The systems can run at higher pressures with less fluid flow so smaller hydraulic lines can be used.

- The direction can be reversed without the use of valves.

The disadvantages of a closed loop are:

- More expensive components are used.

- It may require high-pressure filtration.

- It is more difficult to diagnose faults and repair them.

1.9 Advantages of Hydraulic Systems

1.9.1 High Linear Thrust Power and Power to Weight Ratio

Hydraulic systems transmit energy at high power-to-weight ratios i.e., high forces (torques) can be developed in hydraulic systems with comparatively compact actuators without the need for gearboxes. Hydraulic systems have the highest power linear actuators. This means they can push higher loads at faster speeds than electric or pneumatic actuators.

Hydraulic	Electric	Pneumatic
1400 kN, 350 Bar	25 kN,	30 kN, 7 Bar Air
500 mm / sec, 6000 mm stroke	120 mm / sec, 8500 mm stroke	150 mm / sec, 500 mm stroke

Table 1.2 – Thrust Power as Compared to Other Media

Figure 1.16 - Linear Drive Comparison

Hydraulic Motor

Continuous speed - 8500 rpm

Continuous Power 13 kW

Length - 134 mm

Weight 5 kg

(17.5 hp)

Electric Motor

Speed 3590 rpm

Power 11 kW

Length 320 mm

Weight 65 kg

(15 hp)

Figure 1.17 - Best Power to Weight Ratio

1.9.2   Stall Condition and Overload Protection

A hydraulic actuator can be stalled without damage when it is overloaded and will start up immediately when the load is reduced. The pressure relief valve in a hydraulic system protects it from overload damage.

During a stalled condition or when the load pressure exceeds the valve setting, the pump delivery is directed to the tank with definite limits to torque or force output. The only loss encountered is in terms of pump energy.

On the contrary, stalling an electric motor is likely to cause damage. Likewise, engines cannot be stalled without the necessity for restarting.

High static forces or torques can be achieved and maintained indefinitely. An example is of lifting and keeping lifted, large weights of cargo.

1.9.3 Higher Duty and Longer Life

Provided that the hydraulic fluid is kept perfectly clean, hydraulic systems can also work for much longer or through more cycles than mechanical drives. This is because the metal surfaces never touch as they are always separated by a thin film of fluid.

1.9.4 Accurate Control

The direction of motion, speed and force / torque of hydraulic actuators can easily and accurately be controlled by using components, such as discrete valves, proportional valves and servo valves.

1.9.5 Speed Control

Fully variable speed of both linear and rotary motion, with good "inching" capability and smooth take-up of load; in all cases power is continuously transmitted whilst speed changes take place.

1.9.6 Oily Fluid Medium

As a lubricant, the fluid reduces the friction in the components of a hydraulic system, which helps in prolonging the life of the system components.

1.9.7 Heat Dissipation

The movement of the fluid through a hydraulic system helps to draw heat away from 'hot spots' in the system.

1.10　Disadvantages of Hydraulic Systems

1.10.1　Energy level

Hydraulic systems are high-pressure, high-power systems that require a careful design with all safety precautions.

1.10.2　Contamination

Hydraulic systems need effective control of contamination as they are sensitive to the effects of dirt, moisture and corrosion.

1.10.3　Wear

The components used in hydraulic systems tend to wear, as they are subjected to high forces or torques.

1.10.4　Temperature Dependence

The working of hydraulic systems in extreme temperature conditions deteriorates their performance.

1.10.5　Leakage

A hydraulic system tends to leak because of the defects in its seals. The leakage pollutes the environment besides making the surroundings a mess.

1.10.6　Fire Hazard

There is a risk of fire in a hydraulic system with the mineral-based fluid medium if the leakage of the fluid occurs in the vicinity of a hot environment.

1.10.7 Line Burst

The bursting of hydraulic lines under high pressures can cause injuries to personnel due to high-speed oil jets.

1.10.8 Maintenance

Precision parts of hydraulic systems require good and continuous maintenance, as they are exposed to extreme climates and dirty atmospheres. The fluid media used in these systems also require good filtration to maintain their quality.

1.11 Important Formulae

$$\text{Horsepower} = \frac{\text{GPM x PSI}}{1714}$$

$$\text{Torque (lb. in.)} = \frac{\text{CU IN. / REV. x PSI}}{2\pi}$$

$$\text{Torque (lb. in.)} = \frac{\text{HP x 63025}}{\text{RPM}}$$

$$\text{Flow (gpm)} = \frac{\text{CU IN. / REV. x RPM}}{231}$$

$$\text{Overall efficiency} = \frac{\text{Output HP}}{\text{Input HP}} \times 100$$

$$\text{Volumetric efficiency (pump)} = \frac{\text{Output GPM}}{\text{Theoretical GPM}} \times 100$$

$$\text{Volumetric efficiency (motor)} = \frac{\text{Theoretical GPM}}{\text{Input GPM}} \times 100$$

1.12 Conversion Factors

1 hp = 33,000 ft. lbs. per minute

1 hp = 42.4 btu per minute

1 hp = 0.746 kwhr (kilowatt hours)

1 U.S. gallon = 231 cubic inches.

Pipe volume varies as the square of the diameter; volume in gallons = 0.0034 D^2L

where:

D is the inside diameter of pipe in inches

L is the length in inches

Velocity in feet per second = $\dfrac{0.408 \times \text{flow (gpm)}}{D^2}$

where:

D is the inside diameter of pipe in inches

Atmospheric pressure at sea level = 14.7 PSI

Atmospheric pressure decreases at approximately 0.41 PSI for each one thousand feet of elevation up to 23,000 feet

Pressure (PSI) = feet head x 0.433 x specific gravity.

Specific gravity of oil is approximately 0.85.

Thermal expansion of oil is approximately 1 cu.in. per 1 gal. per 10^OF rise in temperature

1.13 Colour Codes for Fluid Power Schematic Drawings

Colour		Meaning
Black		Intensified pressure
Red		Operating system pressure
Blue		Exhaust – flow without restrictions
Green		Drain / Intake – reservoir to pump
Yellow		Controlled flow
Orange		Pressure lower than system pressure
Violet		Increased fluid pressure
White		System with no pressure

Table 1.3 – Colour Codes for Fluid Power Drawings

1.14 Definitions of Functions

Function	Definition
Intensified Pressure	Pressure in excess of the supply pressure that is induced by a booster or intensifier.
Supply Pressure	Power-actuating fluid.
Charging Pressure	The pump's inlet pressure that is higher than the atmospheric pressure.
Reduced Pressure	The auxiliary pressure which is lower than the supply pressure.
Pilot Pressure	The control-actuating pressure.
Metered Flow	Fluid at the controlled flow rate, other than the pump's delivery.
Exhaust	Return of power and control fluid to the reservoir.
Intake	The sub-atmospheric pressure, usually on the intake side of the pump.
Drain	Return of leakage fluid to the reservoir.

Function	Definition
Inactive	Fluid which is within the circuit, but which does not serve a functional purpose during the phase being represented.

Table 1.4 – Definitions of Functions

***

Chapter 2
Hydraulic Pumps

2.1   Hydraulic Pump

Symbols

A hydraulic pump which is the heart of a hydraulic system, converts mechanical energy from a prime mover into hydraulic energy, which is the combination of pressure and flow that is required by the actuators to perform useful work based on Cosford's Law, which states that:

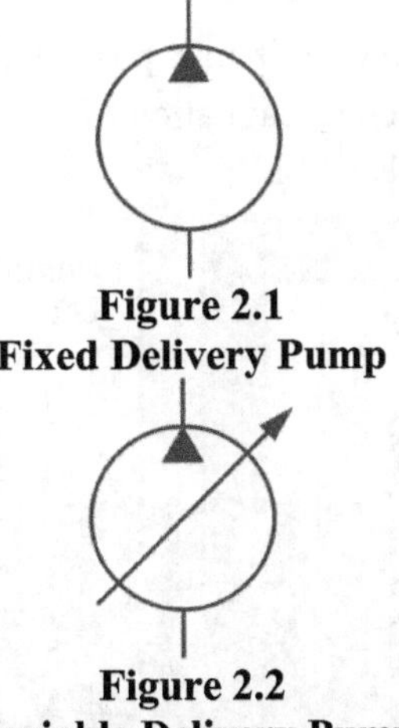

Figure 2.1
Fixed Delivery Pump

Figure 2.2
Variable Delivery Pump

"Pressure makes it go; flow is just the rate at which you can create pressure".

It is important to understand that hydraulic energy is both pressure and flow combined, because one cannot achieve work without the other. A hydraulic pump generates flow with enough power to overcome any pressure induced by the load.

The pump creates a negative pressure at the inlet which causes fluid to be pushed up in the inlet pipe by atmospheric pressure. It results in the fluid lift in the pump suction as shown in the Figure 2.3.

When a hydraulic pump operates, it performs two functions:

a) The pump's mechanical action creates a vacuum at the pump's inlet which allows atmospheric pressure to force liquid from the reservoir into the inlet line to the pump.

b) The pump's mechanical action delivers this liquid to the pump outlet and forces it into the hydraulic system.

Theoretically, a pump lift of 8 m is possible, but it is always lesser due to undesirable effects such as cavitation.

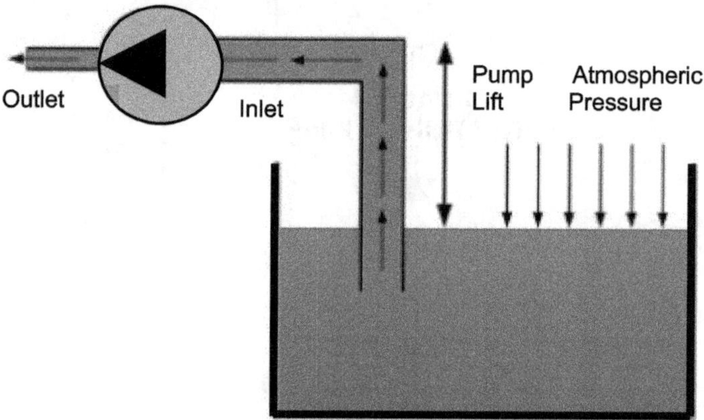

Figure 2.3 – Basic Working Principle of a Hydraulic Pump

The classification of pumps can be either positive displacement or non-positive displacement types. Most pumps used in hydraulic systems are the positive displacement type. A non-positive displacement pump produces a continuous flow, but its output varies considerably as pressure varies because it does not provide a positive internal seal against slippage.

2.2 Positive Displacement Pump

A constant or positive displacement pump, regardless of the pump's rotations per minute, forces a fixed or unvarying quantity of fluid through the outlet port during each revolution of the pump.

It delivers a fixed quantity of fluid per revolution, regardless of the pressure demands. Since the constant-delivery pump provides a fixed quantity of fluid during each revolution of the pump, the quantity of fluid delivered per minute depends upon the pump's rotations per minute.

As mentioned, all pumps operate by creating a partial vacuum at the intake, and a mechanical force at the outlet that induces flow. This action can be best described by reference to a simple piston pump shown in Figure 2.4.

Displacement = Cubic Inches (cc) per Revolution of drive shaft

Flow = Displacement X Shaft Speed X Volumetric Efficiency

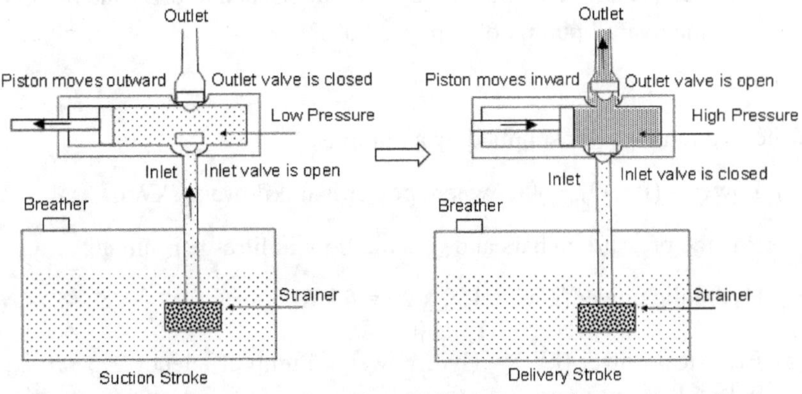

Figure 2.4 - Principle of operation of Positive - Displacement Pumps

As the piston moves to the left, a partial vacuum is created in the pump chamber that holds the outlet valve in place against its seat and induces flow from the reservoir that is at a higher atmospheric pressure. As this flow is produced, the inlet valve is temporarily displaced by the force of fluid, permitting the flow into the pump chamber; this is known as the suction stroke of the pump.

When the piston moves to the right, the resistance at the valves causes an immediate increase in the pressure that forces the inlet valve against its seat and opens the outlet valve thereby permitting the fluid to flow into the system; this is known as the delivery stroke of the pump.

Example

A hydraulic pump delivers 20 L of fluid per minute against a pressure of 250 Bar.

(a) Calculate the hydraulic power.

(b) What size of electric motor would be needed to drive the pump if the overall pump efficiency is 80%?

Solution

The hydraulic power supplied by a pump is:

a) Power = (P x Q) ÷ 600   where power is in kilowatts (kW),

P is the pressure in bars and Q is the flow in litres per minute.

$$\text{Hydraulic power (kW)} = \frac{150 \times 20}{600} = 5 \text{ kW}$$

b) Electrical power (kW) = Hyd. Power ÷ Pump efficiency = 5 ÷ 0.8 = 6.25 KW

All hydraulic pumps are suitable for high pressure applications and small flow rates. These can be classified into rotary and reciprocating type and as per the displacement.

2.2.1   Classification of Hydraulic Pumps

2.2.1.1   Classification Based on The Displacement

- Constant displacement pumps.

  - The flow varies only with the shaft speed

  - Typical types of Gear Pumps and Vane Pumps

- Variable displacement pumps.

  - The flow can be varied at a given shaft speed

  - Typical type is Variable Piston Pumps

2.2.1.2   Classification Based on Construction

Rotary Pump

These pumps displace the oil by means of the rotation of rotors. Gear pumps use gears as rotors and vane pumps have vanes in the radial grooves of the rotor.

The following are the types of rotary pumps:

a) Gear pump

b) Vane pump

c) Screw pump

d) Lobe pump

2.3 Overall Efficiency of Various Types of Hydraulic Pumps

Pump type	Overall Efficiency %	Pump Type	Overall Efficiency %
External Gear	85%	Radial Piston	90%
Internal Gear	90%	Bent Axis Piston	92%
Vane	85%	Axial Piston	91%

Table 2.1 - Overall Efficiency of Hydraulic Pumps

2.4 Rotary Positive Displacement Pumps

2.4.1 Gear Pump

A gear pump uses the meshing and de-meshing of gears to pump fluid by displacement. They are one of the most common types of pumps for hydraulic fluid power applications. Based upon the design, the gear pumps are classified as:

- External gear pumps
- Lobe pumps
- Internal gear pumps
- Gerotor pumps

Figure 2.5
External Gear Pump

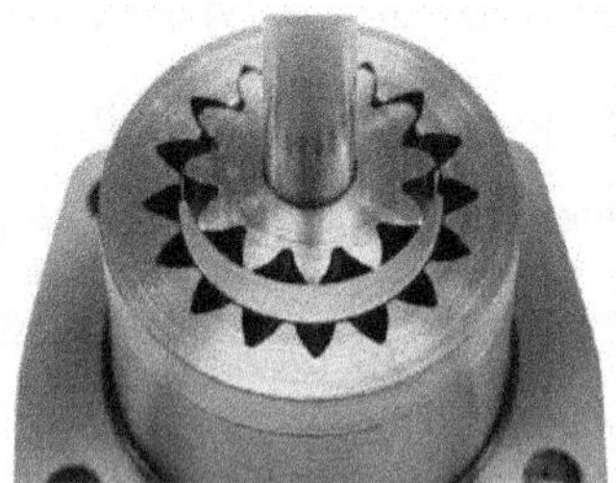

Figure 2.6
Internal Gear Pump

2.4.1.1 External Gear Pump

The external gear pump uses two identical gears rotating against each other. One gear is driven by a prime mover / motor drive shaft and in turn drives the other gear. Each gear is supported by a shaft with bearings on both sides of the gear.

There are three stages in an internal gear pump's working cycle:

1) Filling

2) Transfer

3) Delivery

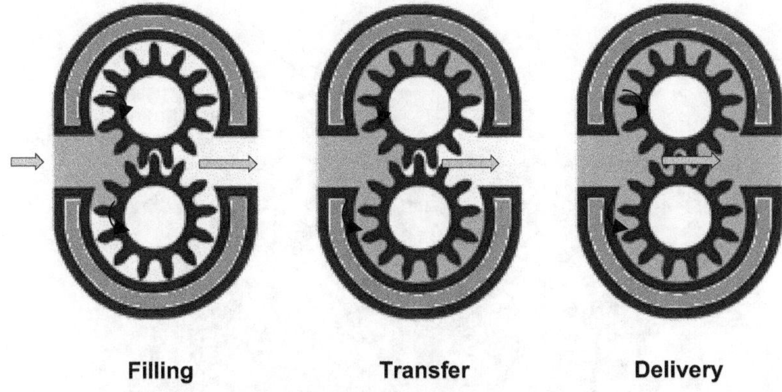

Figure 2.7 - The Working of a Gear Pump

The gears create an expanded volume as they come out of mesh on the inlet side of the pump. Liquid flows into the cavities and is trapped by the gear teeth as the gears continue to rotate against the pump's casing. The trapped fluid is moved from the inlet to the discharge, around the casing.

As the teeth of the gears become interlocked on the discharge side of the pump, the volume is reduced, and the fluid is forced out under pressure.

Close tolerances between the gears and the casing allow the pump to develop suction at the inlet and prevent fluid from leaking back from the discharge side.

Gear pumps are very common in constant flow / constant pressure applications on mobile equipment because of their low cost and dirt tolerance. They are also widely used as charge pumps to pressurize the inlets of piston and vane pumps because of their excellent inlet vacuum tolerance.

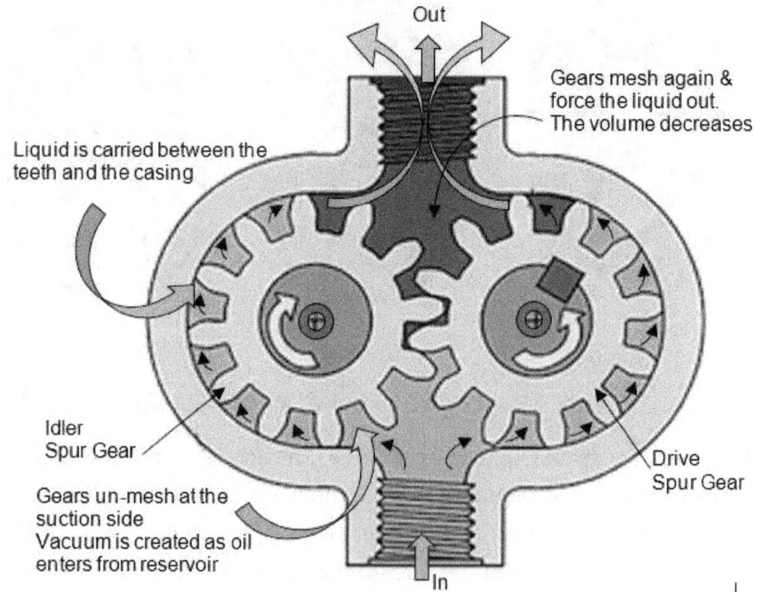

Figure 2.8 - External Gear Pump

2.4.1.2 Lobe Pump

The lobe pump is a close relative of the external gear pump. Two three-lobed, gear shaped units are often used to form the pumping element. However, like an external gear pump, in lobe pumps, the lobes do not make any contact; this is prevented by external timing gears located in the gearbox.

Figure 2.9(a) - Parts of a Lobe Pump

The lobes rotate to create an expanding volume at the inlet like the external gear pump. Now, the fluid flows into the cavity and is trapped by the lobes. Fluid travels around the interior of the casing in the pockets between the lobes and the casing.

Finally, the meshing of the lobes forces liquid to pass through the outlet port. The bearings are placed outside of the pumped liquid. Therefore, the pressure is limited by the bearing location and shaft deflection.

2.4.1.2.1 *Advantages of the Lobe Pump*

✓ It is damage free and often used in food applications because lobe pumps handle solids without any damage to the product.

✓ The particle sizes that can be pumped are often larger in lobe pumps than in other positive displacement pumps

✓ Low viscosity liquids can be handled with diminished performance; there is no metal-to-metal contact.

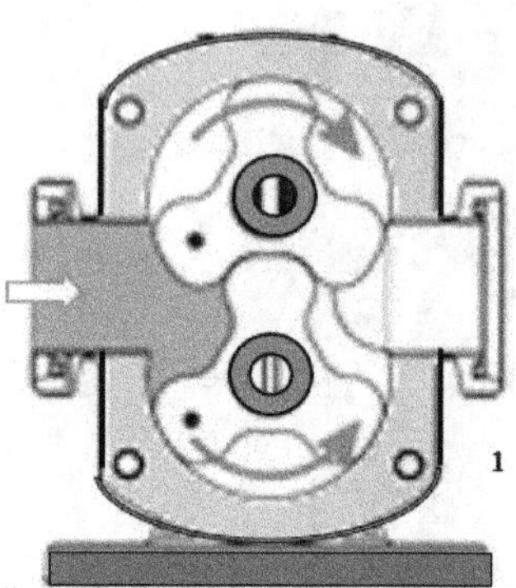

As the lobe is unmeshed, suction is created At the suction side

Fluid is pumped into the pump housing and is trapped by the rotating lobes

Fluids travel around housing and leaves the trapped area.

Meshing of the lobes forces the fluids into the outlet side under pressure.

Figure 2.9(b) - Working of the Lobe Pump

2.4.1.3   *Internal Gear Pump*

It has two gears; one has external teeth and the other has internal teeth. The external gear is inside the internal gear. The two gears are in mesh with each other.

The gear assembly consists of a gear and a pinion. The gear is mounted on and driven by the shaft, and the pinion fitted with a pinion bush and supported on the pinion pin, is driven by the gear.

The centre of the pinion is eccentric to the centre of the gear. A crescent on the casing cover occupies the space between the external circle of the pinion and the internal circle of the gear.

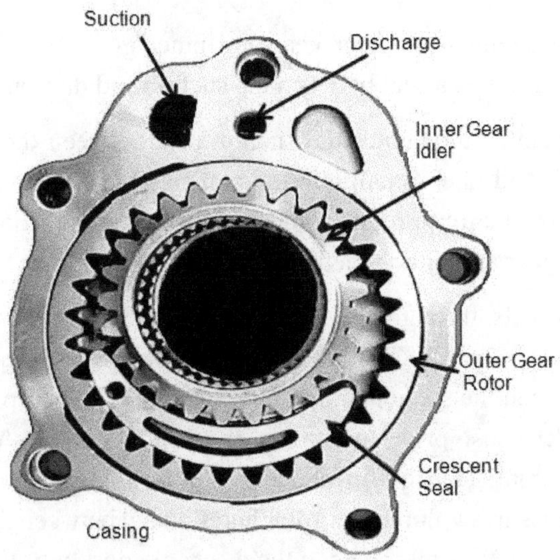

Figure 2.10 - Parts of the Internal Gear Pump

The gear, mounted on the shaft, rotates, and drives the pinion. The pinion rotates inside of the crescent and the gear rotates outside of the crescent. The rotation transfers the oil, which fills in the pockets between the teeth, the crescent seal, and the casing, and is carried along with the gear towards the outlet and is finally delivered at the outlet port.

In addition to superior high-viscosity handling capabilities, internal gear pumps offer a smooth, non-pulsating flow. Internal gear pumps are self-priming and can run dry. As internal gear pumps have only two moving parts, they are reliable, simple to operate, and are easy to maintain. They can operate in either direction which allows for maximum utility with a variety of application requirements.

2.4.1.3.1   Sequence of Working of the Internal Gear Pump

In the beginning, the outer gear and inner gear teeth are perfectly meshed, which act as a seal between the suction and discharge ports.

At this point, fluids enter the suction port between the rotor (large exterior gear) and idler (small interior gear) teeth. As the outer gear and inner gear teeth begin to rotate, fluid is drawn into and floods the space between the gear and pinion teeth.

Liquid travels through the pump between the teeth of the "gear-within-a-gear" principle. The crescent shape divides the liquid and acts as a seal between the suction and discharge ports. The pump head is now nearly flooded, just prior to forcing the liquid out of the discharge port. Intermeshing gears of the idler and rotor form locked pockets for the liquid which assures volume control. Fluid flooded between the outer gear and inner gear teeth is displaced to the discharge port by rotation.

As the outer gear and inner gear teeth begin to mesh again, fluid is pressurized and forced out of the discharge port.

Figure 2.11 - Working of an Internal Gear Pump

2.4.1.4 *Gerotor Pump*

The gerotor pump's name is derived from the words "generated rotor" and is a combination an internal - external gear pump essentially with a housing containing an eccentrically shaped stationary liner.

The inner rotor has n teeth (n > 2), while the outer rotor has n+1 teeth and a pump cover that contains two crescent-shaped openings.

The axis of the inner rotor is offset from the axis of the outer rotor and both rotors rotate on their respective axes.

The geometry of the two rotors partition the space between them into n different dynamically changing volumes during the assembly's rotation cycle; each of these volumes change in a manner such that a given volume first increases and then decreases. An increase creates a vacuum which creates suction and compression occurs when the volume decreases.

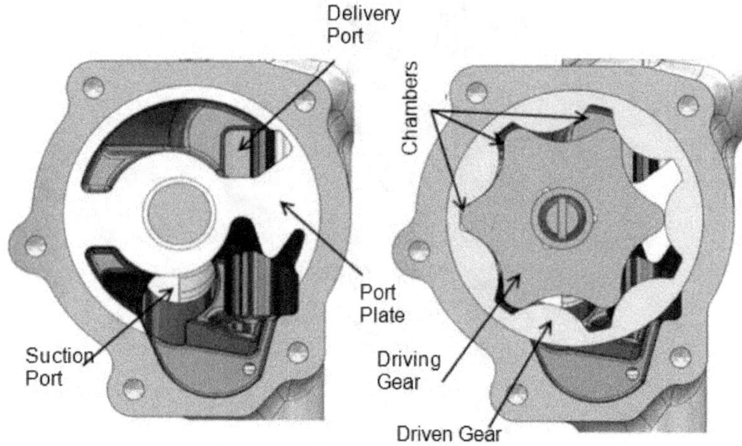

Figure 2.12 - Gerotor Pump

As the inner rotor turns relative to the outer rotor, an increasing volume over the suction port into which fluid is pushed by the atmospheric pressure, is created. As the inner rotor continues to rotate, the suction port is closed, and the supply port opens. At this point the trapped volume starts to decrease, pushing the fluid out of the supply port.

2.4.2 Screw Pump

A screw pump is a positive displacement pump which employs one or multiple screws (generally up to 3), to move fluids from one point to another. Its operation is like that of a gear pump.

2.4.2.1 Working of a Screw Pump

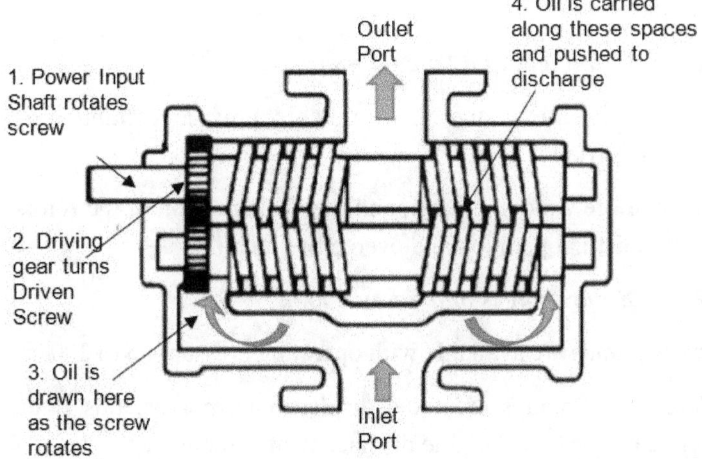

Figure 2.13 - Construction of a Screw Pump

A screw pump can have two or three screw spindles, one of which is a driving gear and the other(s) the driven gear. The gears drive the shafts.

The inlet for the fluid is always located at the bottom and the outlet at the upper part of the pump. The driver and the driven screw rotate in opposite directions or rotate "towards each other", which builds up a suction pressure at the lower part of the pump as the fluid enters from the inlet at the bottom of the pump.

When the screws turn in normal rotation, the fluid contained in these compartments is pushed uniformly along the axis toward the centre of the pump, The fluid crosses the small clearance between the two screws and experiences a centrifugal force. The combination of suction pressure and centrifugal forces the fluid up and out of the pump. To ensure that the discharge pressure does not have a detrimental effect on the life of the screws, there is sometimes a fine hole drilled through the driven screws so that they "float".

2.4.2.2   Advantages of a Screw Pump

1) It is self-priming and more reliable provide continuous (non - pulsating) flow.

2) There are few moving parts, and the rolling action of the rotors make them quiet in operation and even more reliable.

2.4.2.3   Disadvantages of a Screw Pump

1) Screw pumps are available with operating pressure up to 200 bar only.

2) Screw type pumps are fixed displacement pumps; this limits their application where variable displacement is required.

2.4.3   Vane Pump

The disadvantage of a gear pump is the occurrence of a small leakage due to the gap between the gear teeth and the pump housing which is now overcome by the vane pump. The vane-type pump generates a flow using a set of vanes, which are free to move radially within a slotted rotor that rotates in an elliptical chamber. Rotary vane pumps consist of a cylindrical housing, eccentrically positioned rotor, and numerous free-moving vanes. The vanes are placed in the slots of the rotor and, as the rotor turns, the centrifugal force throws the vanes against the cylindrical wall, creating a chamber between the rotor and the cylinder.

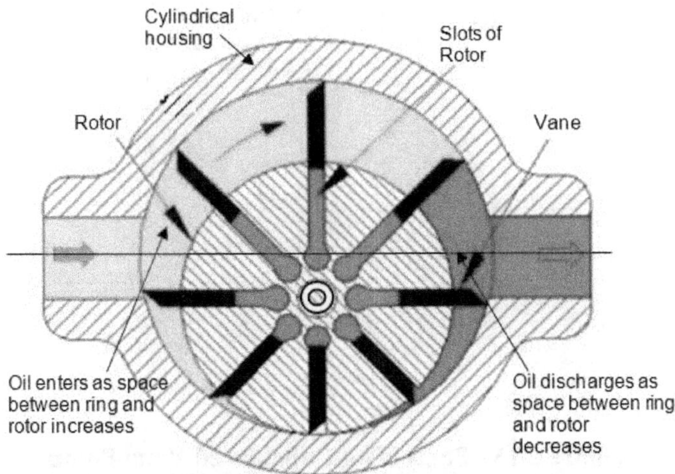

Figure 2.14 - Working Principle of a Vane Pump

The chamber volume changes as the rotor turns from the inlet port, the chamber volume enlarges, and then decreases towards the outlet port.

As oil enters the inlet port and the chamber enlarges, the vanes create a vacuum. And as the oil is pushed through the chamber and it becomes compressed, pressure is produced at the outlet port.

Vane pumps can be hydraulically balanced, which greatly enhance efficiency and are also known for being very quiet during operation and producing very little vibration.

The difference in pressure at the inlet and outlet ports creates a severe load on the vanes and the large side load on the rotor shaft, which leads to an unbalanced load; hence it is called an unbalanced vane pump.

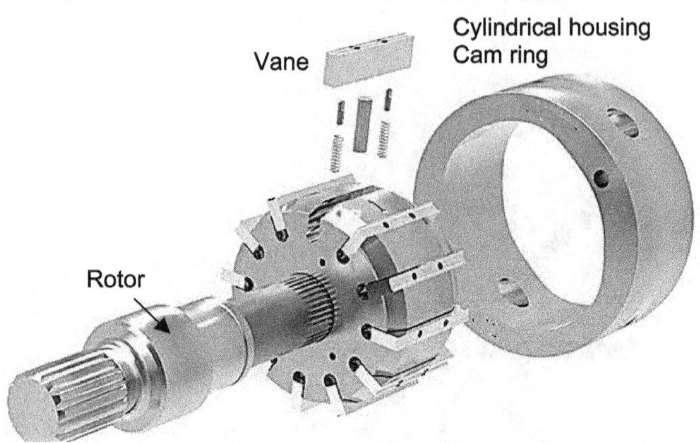

Figure 2.15 - Parts of an Unbalanced Vane Pump

The advantages of vane pumps are as follows:

a) Vane pumps are self-priming, robust and supply constant delivery at a given speed with negligible pulsations

b) These pumps do not require check valves.

c) They are light in weight and compact too.

2.4.3.1 *Balanced Vane Pump*

This pump has an elliptical cam ring with two inlet and two outlet ports.

Pressure loading occurs in the vanes, but the two identical pump halves create equal but opposite forces on the rotor.

It leads to a zero net-force on the shaft and bearings, which increases the life of the pump and the bearing significantly. Hence this pump is called a balanced vane pump

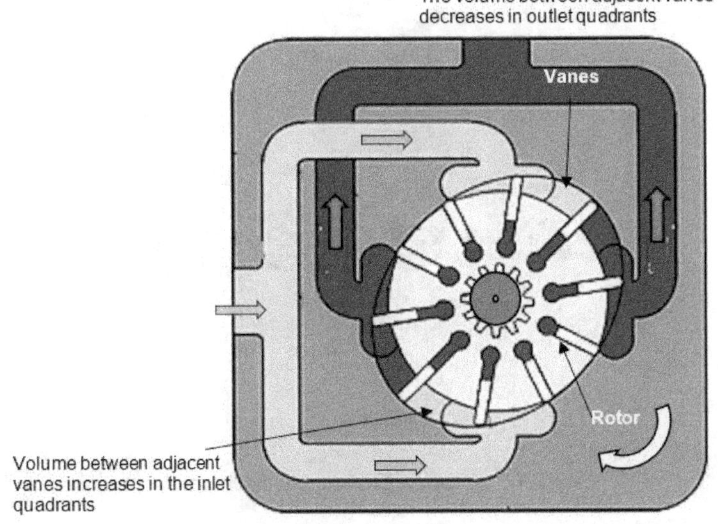

Figure 2.16 - Working of Balance Vane Pump

2.4.3.1.1   Advantages of a Balanced Vane Pump Over an Unbalanced Vane Pump

1) It has a higher flow rate
2) It delivers at a higher pressure and constant volume displacement
3) It has longer life

2.4.3.2   Variable Displacement Vane Pump

With variable displacement, the discharge of the pump can be changed by varying the eccentricity between the rotor and the pump cam-ring.

With a decrease in eccentricity, the discharge decreases; the oil flow also stops when the rotor becomes concentric to the pump's cam ring.

There is no delivery as there is no eccentricity

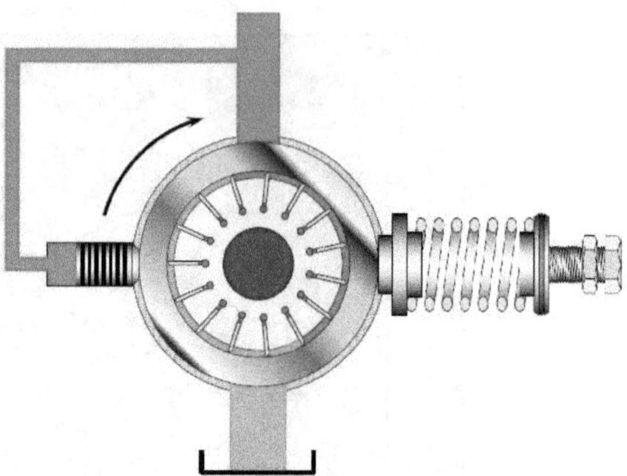

As eccentricity increases, the pump's discharge increases.

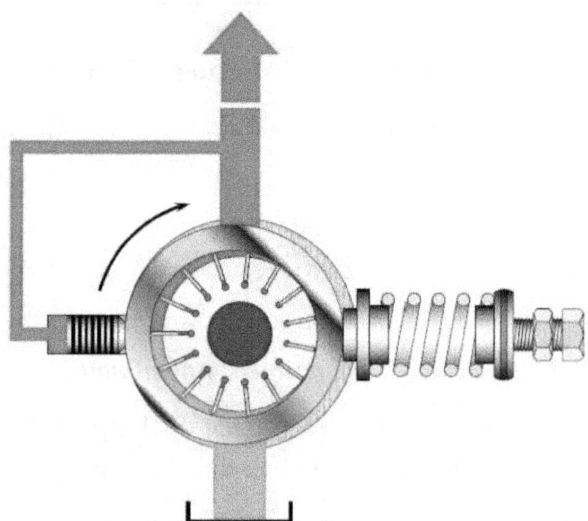

Figure 2.17 - Working of a Variable Displacement Vane Pump

2.5   Piston / Reciprocating Pump

These pumps displace the medium by a reciprocating motion of the plungers / pistons.

The piston pump uses the principle of a reciprocating pump to produce fluid flow. This pump has many piston-cylinder combinations instead of using a single piston. Part of the pump mechanism rotates about a drive shaft to generate the reciprocating motion, which draws fluid into each cylinder and then expels it thus producing flow.

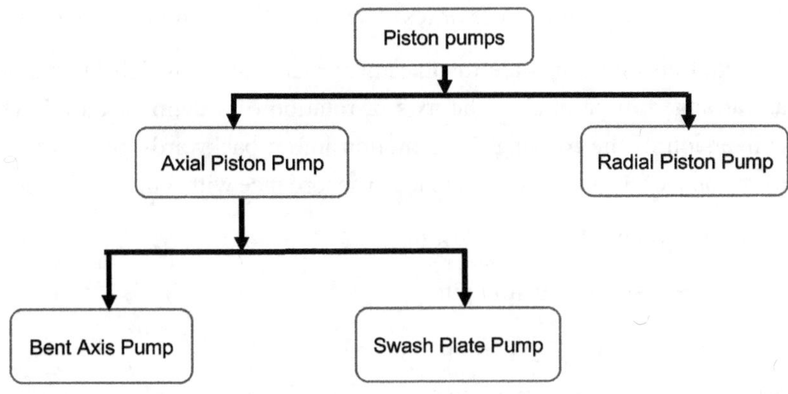

Figure 2.18 - Types of Piston Pumps

Hydraulic piston pumps can handle large flows at high system pressures. The piston pump is a hydraulic pump that delivers with optimum efficiency and reliability while maintaining a compact size and a high-power density. In these pumps, the pistons accurately slide back and forth inside the cylinders that are part of the hydraulic pump. The sealing properties of the pistons are excellent, which makes it possible to operate at high pressures with low fluid leakage.

The displacement of a piston pump can be easily calculated as follows:

Q = (number of pistons) × (piston area) × (piston stroke) × (drive speed)

2.5.1 *Axial Piston Pump*

It can be used as a stand-alone pump. An axial piston pump usually has an odd number of pistons arranged in a circular array within a housing, which is commonly referred to as a cylinder block, rotor, or barrel.

This cylinder block is driven to rotate about its axis of symmetry by an integral shaft that is more or less aligned with the pumping pistons.

Axial piston pumps are displacement machines in which the pistons are arranged in parallel to the axis of rotation of a cylinder barrel. The conversion of the rotating drive motion into a backwards and forwards movement of the pistons takes place in accordance with 3 main principles.

These pumps are of two designs:

1) Swash-plate piston pump

2) Bent-axis piston pump

2.5.1.1 *Swash-Plate Type Piston Pump*

A swashplate is a device that works similar to a crankshaft and is used to translate the motion of a rotating shaft into a reciprocating motion.

A swash-plate piston pump is an axial piston pump in which the pistons reciprocate parallel to the axis of rotation of the cylinder block, as the cylinder block and drive shaft are located on the same centre line.

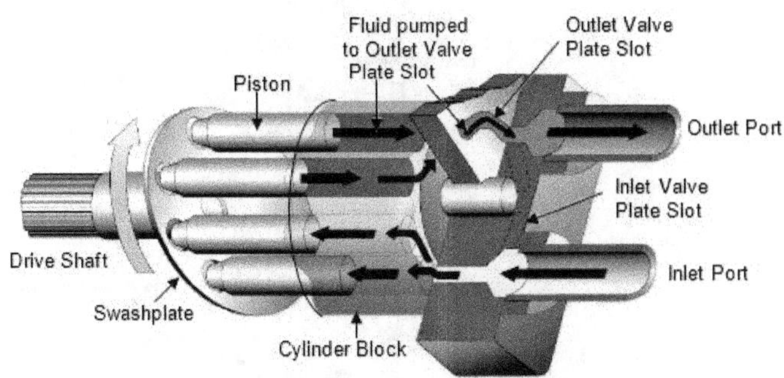

Figure 2.19 - Parts of Axial Piston Pump

The cylinder block is driven by the drive shaft in a fixed position. The pistons, which are fitted into cylinders in the drive block, are connected by piston shoes to the angled swash plate. The working principle of a swash-plate type piston pump is described as follows:

The outlet and inlet ports are in the valve plate so that the pistons pass the inlet as they are being pulled out and pass the outlet as they are being forced back in.

During the suction phase, the pistons move out of the barrel and are forced against the swash plate by a special retaining plate.

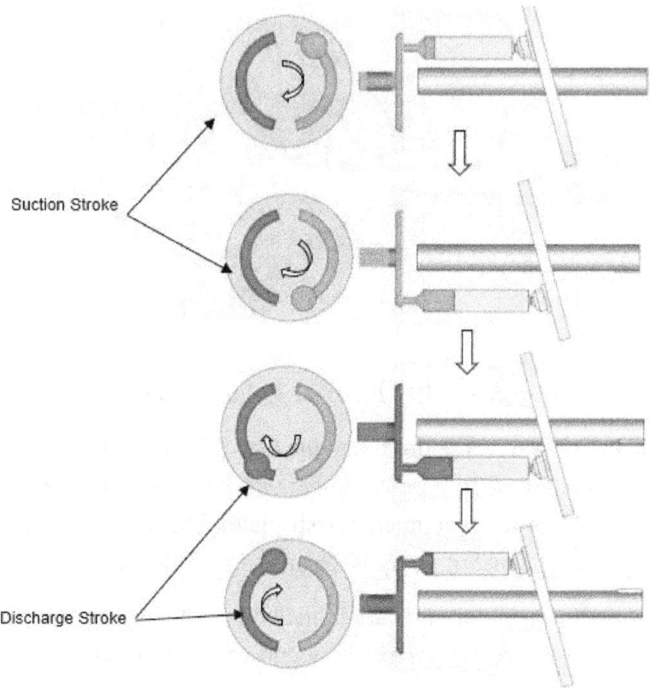

During the discharge phase, the swash plate forces the pistons back into the barrel.

Figure 2.20 - Working of Swash-Plate-Type Piston Pump

As the block rotates, the shoes follow the course of the swash plate, causing the pistons to reciprocate within the cylinders.

As the pistons move outwards, a suction port is formed, and oil is drawn into the cylinders.

The ports are arranged in the valve plate so that the pistons pass the inlet as they are pulled out and pass the outlet as they are forced back in as the cylinder rotates.

The pistons reciprocate because the piston shoes follow the angled surface of the swash plate. As the pistons continue to rotate, they move inwards due to the angle of the swash plate, thus discharging oil. The discharge and inlet ports are located in the valve plate.

2.5.1.1.1 *Variable Delivery Swash - Plate Piston Pump*

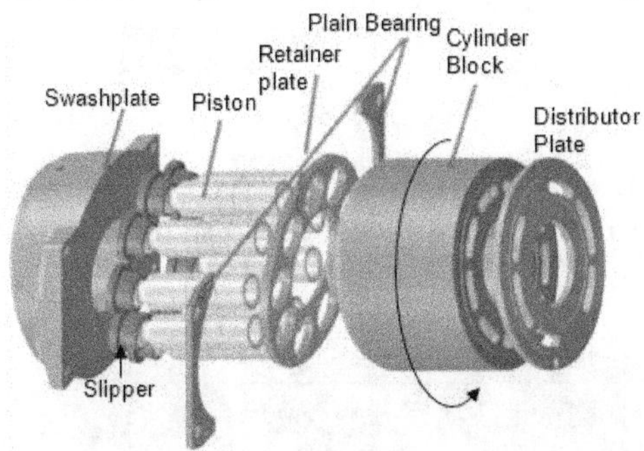

Figure 2.21 - Parts of Swash-Plate-Type Piston Pump

The displacement of swash plate axial piston pumps is determined by the size and number of pistons, as well as the stroke length.

Q = (No. of Pistons) x (Piston Size) x (Piston Stroke) x (Drive Speed)

The stroke length is determined by the angle of the swash plate and the maximum angle is limited to 17.5°.

Any displacement between zero and maximum is easily achieved with relatively simple actuators to change the swash plate angle.

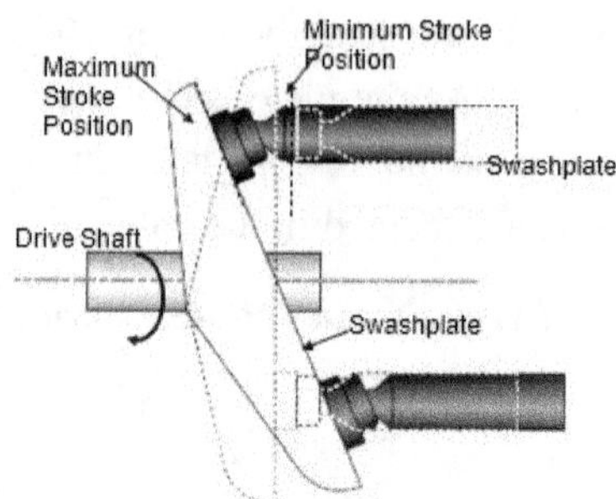

Figure 2.22

Variable Delivery Swash Plate-Type Piston Pump

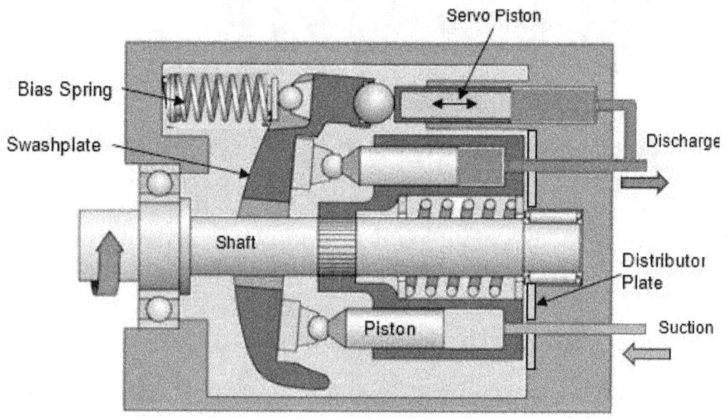

Figure 2.23 - Parts of Variable Delivery Swash -Plate-Type Piston Pump

2.5.1.1.2 *Variable Displacement Pressure Compensated Hydraulic Pump*

A pressure compensator control device maintains the set pressure and is built into a variable delivery hydraulic pump as shown in Figure 2.24. It protects the pump when it is overloaded (if the system pressure sensed on the pump's outlet port should rise above a pre-set desired maximum pressure). It thus by reduces the pump's outlet flow automatically.

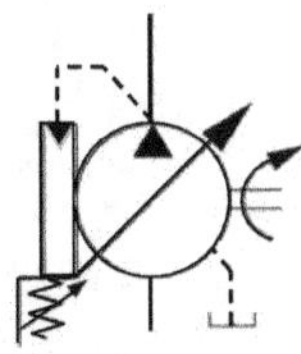

Figure 2.24

A pressure-compensated pump will thus provide a full pump flow at pressures below the compensator setting. Once the pump flow is restricted, pressure will build up to the setting of the compensator and then the pump will de-stroke to the level needed to maintain the compensator's pressure setting.

A variable displacement pressure-compensated hydraulic pump's outlet pressure is controlled by the swashplate angle, which is in turn, controlled by the compensator control valve and servo piston as shown in Figure 2.25.

The compensator acts with the help of hydraulic pressure that is obtained internally from the pump's outlet port and its compensator spool is positioned based on a force-balance between the compensator chamber's pressure acting on the piston and spring's force. The spring in the compensator can be adjusted for the maximum desired pressure. Normally, at low system pressures, the swash plate remains at its maximum angle, held there by the spring's force.

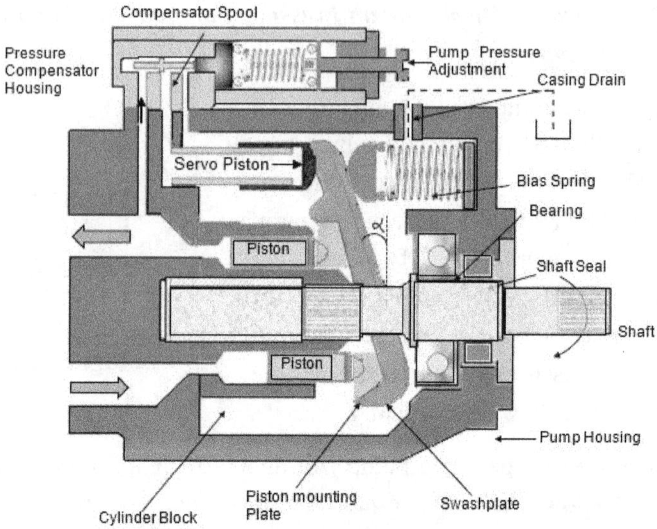

Figure 2.25 - Parts of Variable Displacement Pressure Compensated Hydraulic Pump

When the pump pressure rises high enough to overcome the adjustable spring behind the compensator piston, the compensator control valve will shift to supply oil pressure to the servo piston. Due to the surface area of the servo piston and the pressure exerted on that area, a force is generated that pushes the swash plate of the pump to a lower degree of the stroke angle. The servo piston will start to pull the swash plate back towards the neutral position, causing the piston travel in the rotating group to be reduced, thus reducing the pump's displacement and output flow.

Once the pressure in the system drops below the compensator setting, the compensator spool is forced back in the other direction via the spring force. This allows the oil in the servo piston chamber to exhaust into the case of the pump, where it is returned to the tank via a drain line.

The servo piston force that was holding the swash plate at a low angle is now reduced and the bias spring pushes the swash plate back onto its stroke at a full angle and flow. The pump tries to maintain the compensator's set pressure and will provide flow up to its maximum flow rate to reach that pressure setting. Most hydraulic systems work very well with the pump compensator setting of about 10 to 13 bar above the maximum load pressure and the relief valve set at about 17 to 20 bar above the compensator's setting. This is to ensure that the relief valve is set above its cracking pressure to avoid dumping across it, wasting energy, and generating heat while moving heavy loads. Variable displacement pumps are useful in hydraulic systems where several branch circuits are to be supplied from one pump, where maximum pressure may be required simultaneously in more than one branch and where the pump must be unloaded when none of the branches is in operation. As shown in the Figure 2.26, a 4-way closed-centre-spool direction control valve is used in each branch. The inlet ports on all 4-way valves are connected in parallel across the pump's discharge pressure line.

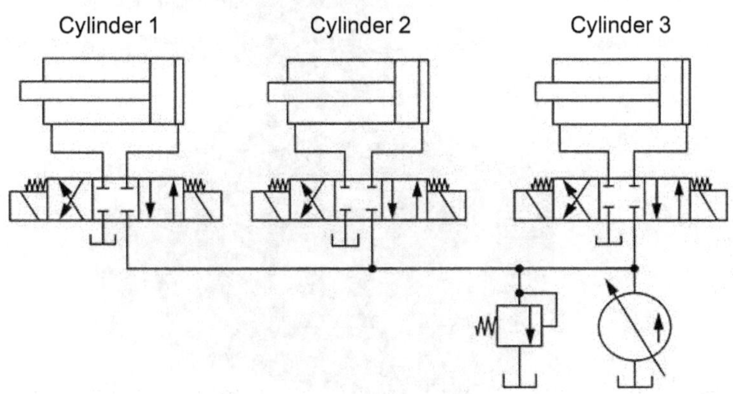

Figure 2.26 - Application of Variable Displacement

Pressure Compensated Pump

A pressure-compensating pump will deliver its maximum flow until the system pressure reaches the compensator's setting. Once the compensator's setting is reached, the pump will be de-stroked to deliver only the amount of flow that will maintain the compensator's setting in the line. Whenever more flow is demanded by the system when an additional actuator is in use, the pump will increase its stroke to meet the new flow demand. Whenever the system flow needs to decrease when one or more actuators are stopped, the pump stroke is reduced.

When the system is stopped completely, the pump stroke is reduced almost to zero. It will stroke only a very small amount or whatever is required to maintain the compensator's setting in the line, overcoming any system by-passing or leaks. While a pressure-compensating pump is efficient, the standby pressure remains high, which will heat up the fluid due to waste energy.

2.5.1.1.3 *Pressure-Flow Compensated Variable Volume Piston Pump*

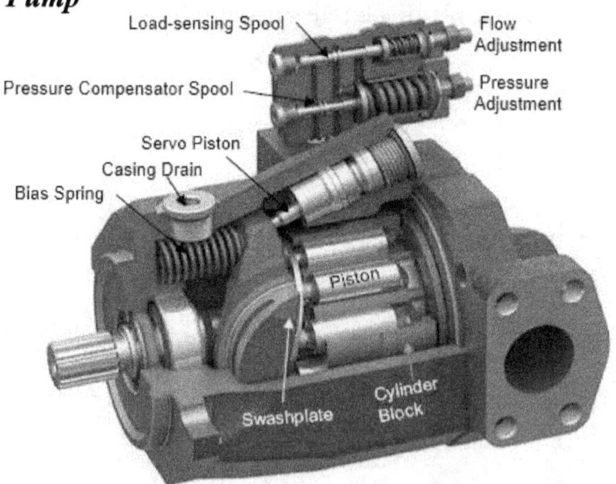

Figure 2.27 - Load sensing Variable Displacement

Pressure Compensated Pump

A pump used in a typical load-sensing hydraulic circuit will still have a pressure compensator for limiting the maximum system pressure; a second control device is used to provide fine control over the pump's displacement and the system pressure during normal working parameters.

A load-sensing control has a conventional pressure compensating action; it also has a flow compensator which responds to the volume of flow that is permitted to pass through the system's flow control valve and keeps the pump's displacement always reduced to this exact amount and under all conditions of loading.

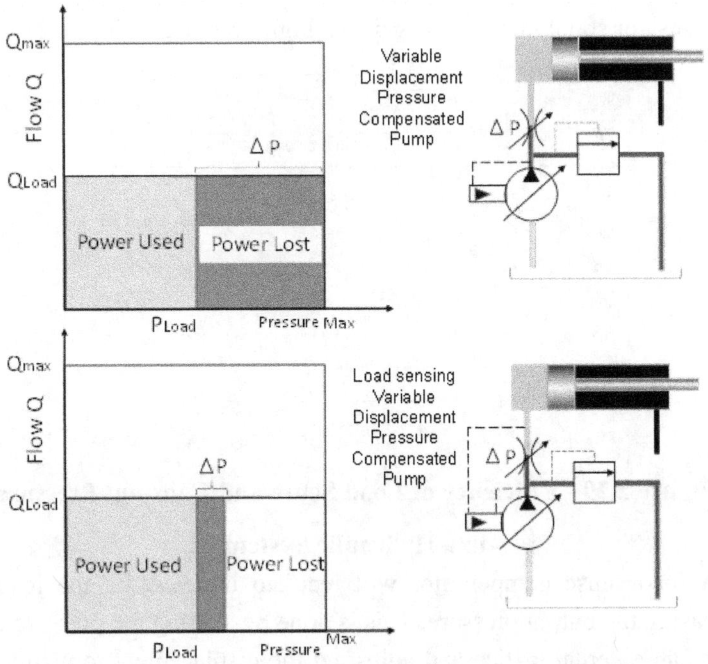

Figure 2.28 - Comparison between Only Pressure Compensated and Pressure Compensated with Flow Compensation

The total action of the controller is to regulate the piston pump's swashplate angle so that the pump will produce only the flow needed and at only the pressure required by the load.

Thus, the controlling of both pressure and flow compensation results in the most efficient use of input power, the most precise control of the fluid power and the least amount of oil heating of any system devised to date. The load sensing system for the control of a hydraulic actuator consists of a variable-displacement pump with a compensator block which consists of a pressure-flow compensator spool that works against a low-pressure spring of 20 bar, for example, and a high-pressure compensator spool that works against a high-pressure spring of 250 bar.

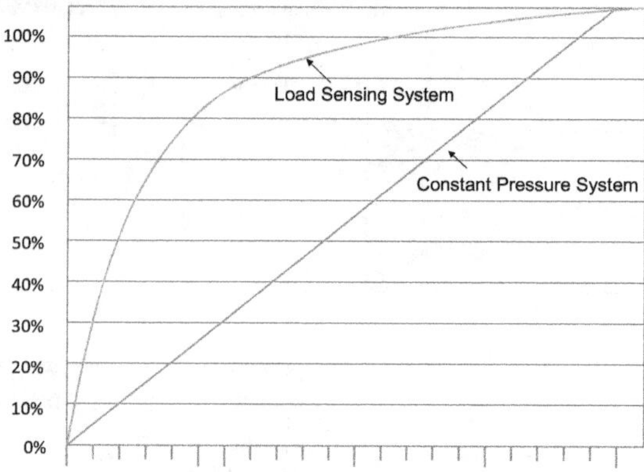

Figure 2.29 - Efficiency of Load Sense and Constant Pressure

in a Hydraulic System

A load sense compensator will react to increases in the load by increasing the output pressure. This is done by sensing the pressure drop across an external orifice and adjusting the displacement to maintain a constant pressure drop across the orifice.

The compensator, when connected to a hydraulic system, senses the pressure and the flow conditions of the system. The pump will produce a flow, trying to balance the load pressure plus the differential spring against the pump's outlet pressure.

2.5.1.2   Modes of Operation a Load Sense Axial Piston Pump

When the pump is switched on, the system will slip into the following modes namely:

a)   Low-pressure Stand-by Mode

When the pump is on and the directional control valve is in its centre position, it is in this mode.

b)   Load-sensing Mode

When the directional control valve is actuated and the load is moving with the requirement of pressure and flow, it is in this mode.

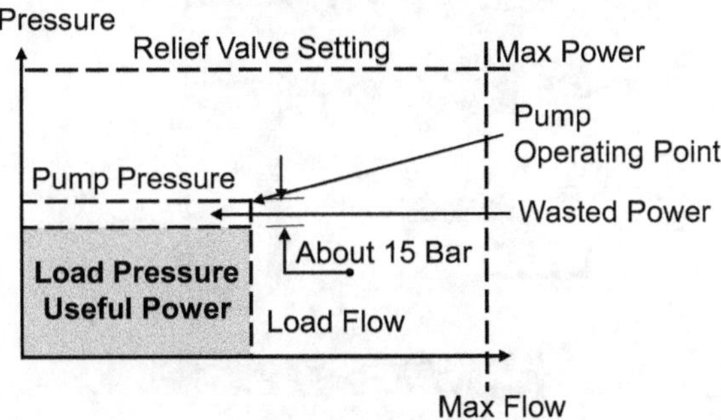

Figure 2.30 - Pressure vs Flow of a Load Sense Axial Piston Pump

2.5.1.2.1 *High-Pressure Stand-By Mode During Its Cycle of Operation*

When the load comes to a stand-still under pressurized condition, it is in this mode.

2.5.1.2.2 *Initial Condition*

The 20-bar spring of the compensator forces the pressure-flow compensator spool towards the right when there is no pressure in the system. This normal position of the spool provides a direct passage for the fluid to flow from the swashplate control piston to the reservoir. As there is no fluid pressure acting on the control piston of the pump, the swash plate of the pump is forced to move to its maximum angle position. In this position, the pump is ready to produce the maximum flow.

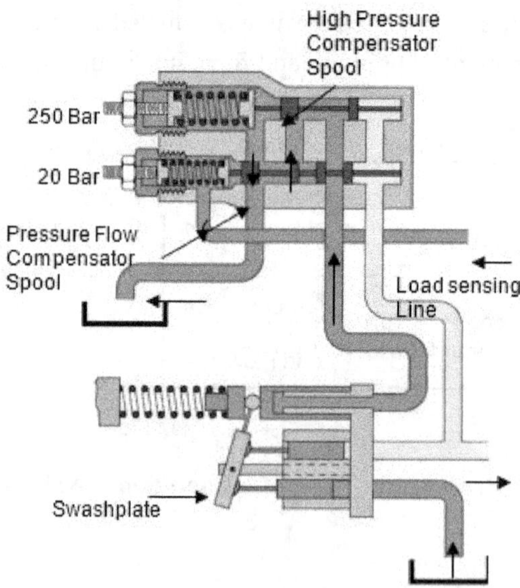

Figure 2.31 – The Swash Plate at its Maximum Angle

2.5.1.2.3   Low-Pressure Standby Mode

When the pump is switched on and the flow to the actuator is blocked by the closed-centre directional control valve, the pressure-flow compensator spool moves to the left against the low-pressure spring as soon as the pressure reaches 20 bar.

The pressure-flow compensator spool allows the fluid flow to be directed to the swashplate control piston, which causes the swashplate to de-stroke and make the pump to deliver a minimal flow at the low pressure to the idling system, for making up the internal leakages. This position of the system is regarded as the low-pressure standby mode.

2.5.1.2.4   Load Sensing Mode

The reason that this flow control is so important is because there must be a constant pressure difference between the pump outlet pressure and the load sense pressure. This difference will be equal to the spring-setting of the load sense compensator which is known as the margin pressure. A load sense compensator will react to increases in the load by increasing the output pressure. This is done by sensing the pressure drop across an external orifice and adjusting the displacement to maintain a constant pressure drop across the orifice. When a load (resistance) is suddenly added to the motor, it will slow down as the pressure rise also has the added effect of decreasing the pressure differential across the flow control device. The added resistance will cause the hydraulic pressure to rise, and this rise is detected back at the pump through the load sense line.

The increase of the load sense pressure forces the load sense compensator valve to open which will create a flow path that allows fluid from the internal control piston to escape into the pump casing and from there out through the case drain line to the tank.

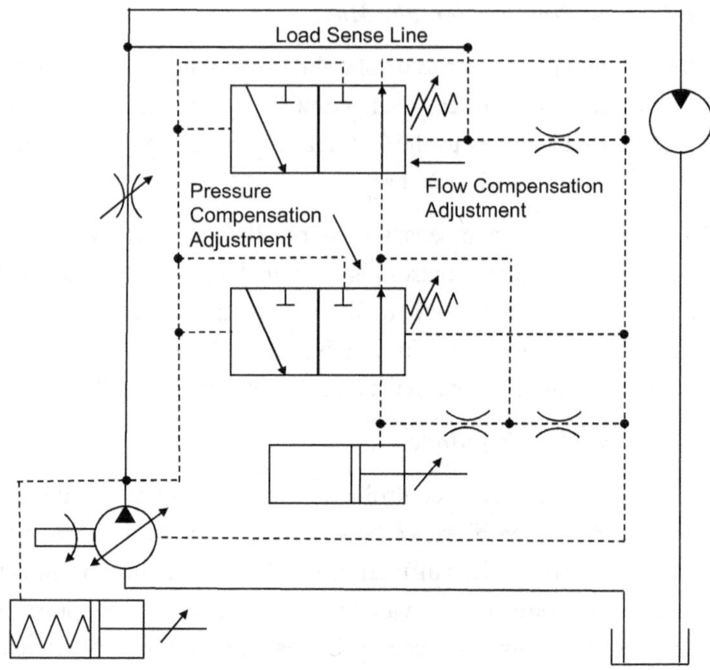

Figure 2.32 - Load Sensing Control of a Variable Displacement Pressure Compensated Pump

As the fluid leaves the control piston, the bias spring pushes the swash plate further on stroke, increasing the pump's displacement. This causes the pump's output pressure to rise and forces the load sense compensator valve to close again.

If the load pressure increases, the pump outlet pressure will increase proportionately to maintain a constant pressure drop across the orifice, but since the load sense control is working to maintain a constant pressure drop across the orifice, the load sense pump will de-stroke to maintain the same output flow.

Therefore, in a load sense circuit, the pump will maintain the same output flow, independent of the pump's drive speed.

As shown in Figure 2.32, most load sense controls also incorporate a pressure limiter feature which limits the maximum pressure that the pump will achieve.

Once the load pressure reaches the setting of the max pressure spring, the poppet lifts off the seat and limits the pressure in the differential spring chamber. As outlet pressure increases it will shift the spool and de-stroke the pump.

Load sensing is an ideal hydraulic system when the system requires one or more of the following characteristics:

- One system pump to operate multiple circuits with variable pressures and flow.

- A system that requires a constant flow rate regardless of input RPM and variable pressure requirements.

- A system that requires variable flow rates.

- A system that will standby at low pressure and low flow until pressure or flow is required.

- A system that drives hydraulic motors at constant speed regardless of load.

- A system that does not waste excessive energy and create excessive system heat.

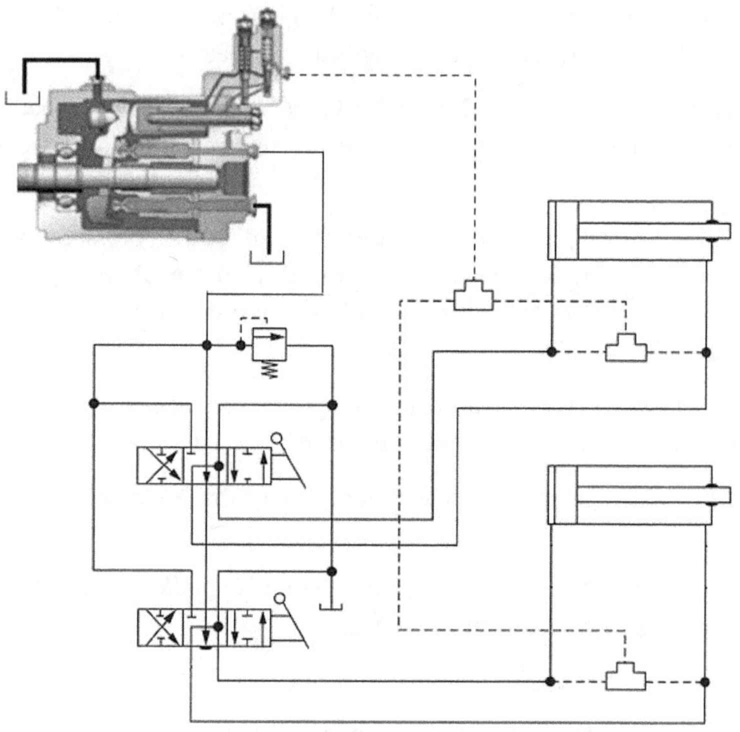

Figure 2.33 - Pressure and Flow Compensation

for a Pump with Multiple Load Sensing Control

2.5.1.3   *Bent Axis Hydraulic Pump*

In a bent axis piston type of hydraulic pump, the cylinder block turns with the drive shaft, but at an offset angle. The angular housing of the pump causes a corresponding angle to exist between the cylinder block and the drive shaft plate to which the pistons are attached. It is this angular configuration of the pump that causes the pistons to stroke as the pump shaft is turned.

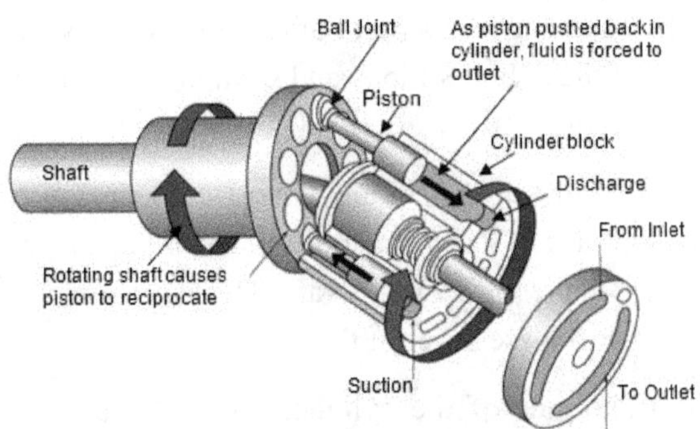

Figure 2.34 - Bent Axis Piston Pump

When the pump operates, all parts within the pump except for the outer races of the bearings that support the drive shaft, the cylinder bearing pin on which the cylinder block turns, and the oil seal, turn together as a rotating group. At one point of rotation of this rotating group, a minimum distance exists between the top of the cylinder block and the upper face of the drive shaft plate.

Figure 2.35 – Pictorial View of a Bent Axis Pump

As the angled housing is at a point of rotation 180° away, the distance between the top of the cylinder block and the upper face of the drive shaft plate is at a maximum.

At any given moment of operation, three of the pistons are moving away from the top face of the cylinder block, producing a partial vacuum in the bores in which these pistons operate. This occurs over the inlet port, so fluid is drawn into these bores at this time.

On the opposite side of the cylinder block, three different pistons move towards the top face of the block. This occurs while the rotating group is passing over the outlet port thereby causing fluid to be expelled from the pump by these pistons.

The continuous and rapid action of the pistons is overlapping in nature and results in a practically non-pulsating pump output.

In contrast to the swash plate design, the stroke movement of the pistons is achieved by the inclined position of the cylinder drum to the drive shaft, or the displacement volume changes in accordance with this pivot angle.

The displacement of this type of pump varies with the offset angle, the maximum angle being 30 degrees and the minimum being zero. Fixed-displacement bent axis pumps are usually available with 23-degree or 30-degree angles.

In the variable-displacement construction, a yoke with an external control is used to change the angle. With some controls, the yoke can be moved over the centre to reverse the direction of flow.

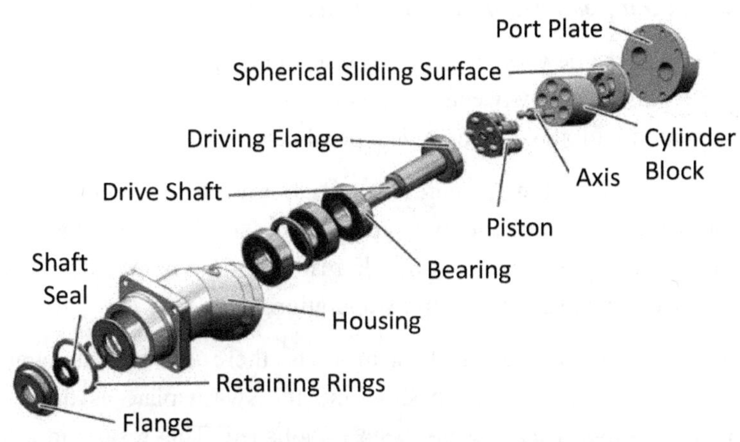

Figure 2.36 - Parts of Fixed Bent Axis Pump

2.5.1.4   Comparison of Bent Axis versus Swash Plate

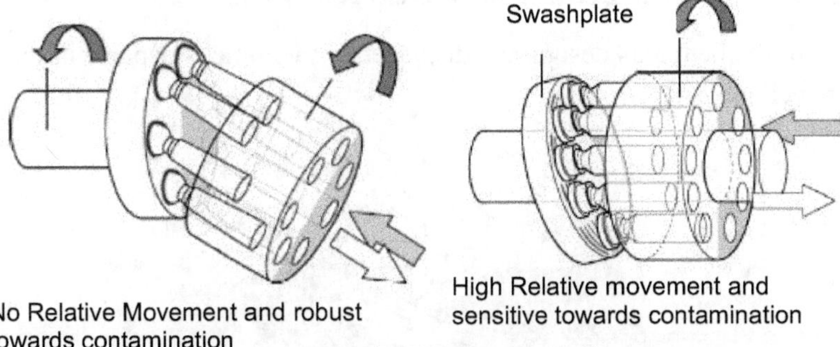

No Relative Movement and robust towards contamination

High Relative movement and sensitive towards contamination

Figure 2.37 - Bent Axis Pump

Figure 2.38 - Swashplate Pump

Some Special Features of the Swashplate Pump

a) The oil has to be very clean as this type of pump has a relatively high-speed movement between the piston shoes and the swash plate as compared with the oblique-axis type of piston pump.

b) As it is a through-drive pump, it has an advantage of others and as compared to the oblique axis type, the swash plate pump has a low moment of inertia, and its variable response time is fast, which is in fact advantageous to the pump's operation.

c) Once the swash plate mechanism starts, there is a high amount of friction between the piston shoe and the swash plate as the static pressure support has yet not been established. This results in a low starting torque; thus, an inclined axis is preferred when the starting is frequent.

2.5.1.5 Variable Delivery Bent Axis Piston Pump

In the bent axis design, the displacement volume is dependent on the swivel angle.

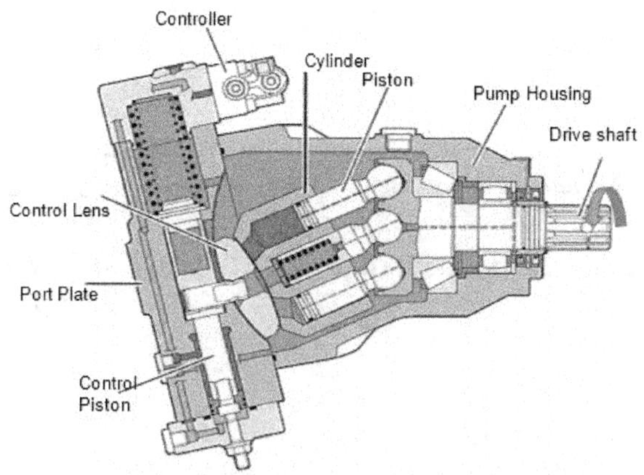

Figure 2.39 - Variable Delivery Bent Axis Piston Pump

Various methods are used to control the displacement of bent-axis pumps; typically, control is achieved with the manually controlled pressure compensator.

2.5.1.6 *Pressure Compensator Control of Bent-Axis Pump*

As shown in Figure 2.40, when the system pressure is high enough to overcome the spring force set by the pressure compensator setting, the piston pushes the spool up. As a result, the spool lifts, allowing fluid to flow into the stroking cylinder.

Although the holding cylinder also has the system pressure applied, the area of the stroking cylinder piston is much greater. Due to the differential pressure, the yoke is forced up to decrease flow and thus pressure compensation is achieved.

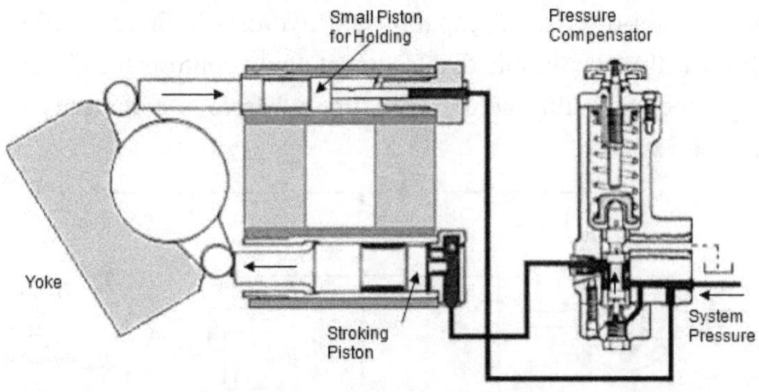

Figure 2.40 - Pressure Compensator Control of Bent-Axis Pump

2.5.1.7   Bi-directional Variable Displacement Hydraulic Pump

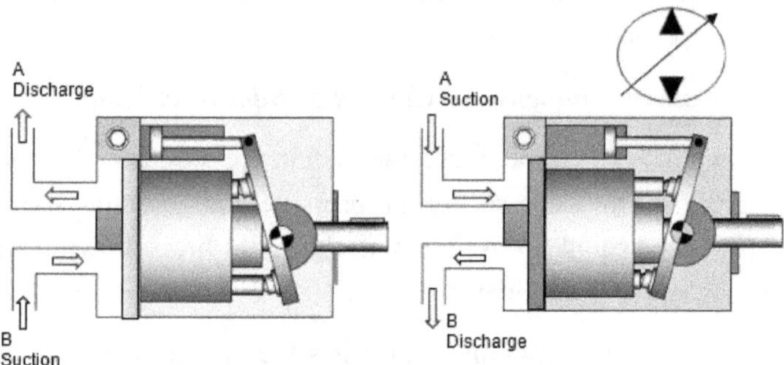

Figure 2.41 - Bi-directional Variable Displacement Hydraulic Pump

When one or more hydraulic motors need to be driven at variable speeds with bi-directional capability, a hydrostatic drive is often used. The bi-directional, variable displacement pump controls the direction and speed of the hydraulic motor. This type of drive is commonly called a closed-loop system.

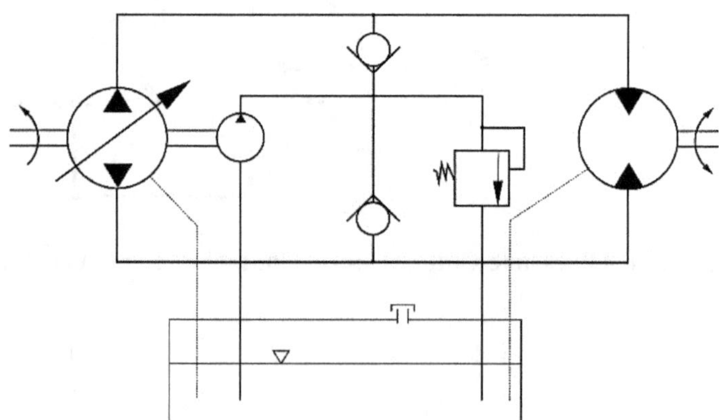

Figure 2.42 - Closed Loop Hydraulic System

We know that a closed loop hydrostatic hydraulic system is one in which the oil flows from the pump to the hydraulic motor and back to the pump.

This type of hydraulic system gives immediate control over power functions associated within the system's loop, including the pause / resume speed control feature of hydraulic motors.

2.5.1.8   Main Pump

An axial piston pump is used in a hydrostatic transmission whose volume can be varied from minimum to maximum by changing the swashplate angle, for example when it is in the vertical position, which means that the pump output is at 0 LPM.

The swashplate is moved by two internal cylinders, which are controlled by a separate valve or manual lever. The amount the swashplate angles in each direction determines the flow from the pump.

The swashplate will change its angle and deliver fluid out of the "A" port, and the "B" port will act as the suction port to drive the hydraulic motor forward. The oil that exhausts out of the hydraulic motor, will flow into the "B" port.

To drive the motor in the reverse direction, the swashplate will change its angle in the opposite direction. The "B" port will then be the pressure port, and the "A" port will be the suction, as seen in Figure 2.41.

2.5.1.8.1   Charge Pump

In a closed loop hydraulic system, a charge pump is mounted on the back end of the main pump; it has a volume normally of about 10 to15% of the main pump as shown in Figure 2.43.

When the main pump is idle, the charge pump's volume flows through the charge pump's relief valve that provides a flow path for the excess volume to return to the tank in the idle mode.

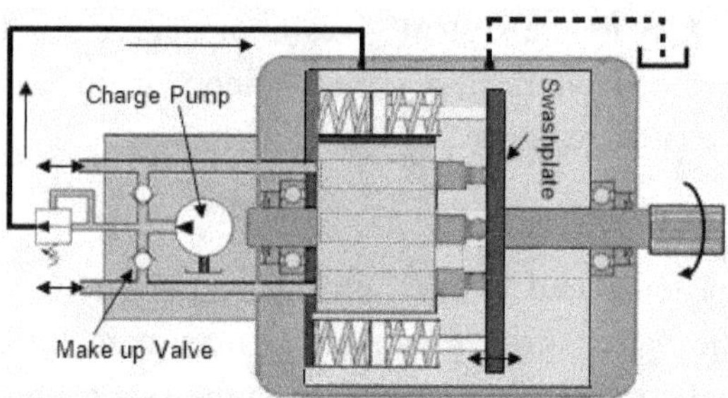

Figure 2.43 - Charge Pump in closed loop Hydraulic System

The relief valve is normally mounted on or near the charge pump. The outlet flow of this relief valve is usually ported into the pump's case, where it returns to the tank through the main pump's case drain line.

The purpose of the charge pump is to provide "make-up fluid" to the system when it is operating.

The charge pump will supply the make-up oil through the check valve, thereby preventing pump cavitation. In this type of system, the power piston is used as a stroking cylinder to control the main pump's swash plate angle; the charge pump also supplies the fluid to the stroking cylinders.

2.5.1.8.2 *Make-up Check Valves*

Make-up check valves permit free flow from the charge pump to the low-pressure side of the loop. At the same time, oil in the high-pressure side is blocked to the low-pressure side by the opposite check valve. The check valves are normally accessed by removing the charge pump.

2.5.1.8.3   Cross Port Relief Valves

Cross port relief valves limit the maximum pressure in the system. If the motor should mechanically stall, the relief valve on the high-pressure side would open and dump fluid back to the low-pressure side of the loop, protecting the motor from over pressurising.

The valves also absorb shock spikes in the system. To best absorb the pressure spikes, the valves are generally mounted as close to the motor as possible.

The valves are pre-set above the maximum operating pressure. Some drives may have a maximum pressure override, which operates similarly to a pump compensator. When the pressure override setting is reached, the pump volume is reduced to an output of nearly zero litres per minute.

The pump will only deliver enough oil to maintain the pressure override setting. On these systems, the pressure override is set below the cross-port relief valve settings. The speed and direction of the motor is determined by the variable displacement hydraulic pump.

The maximum pressure to the motor is controlled by the cross-port relief valve settings.

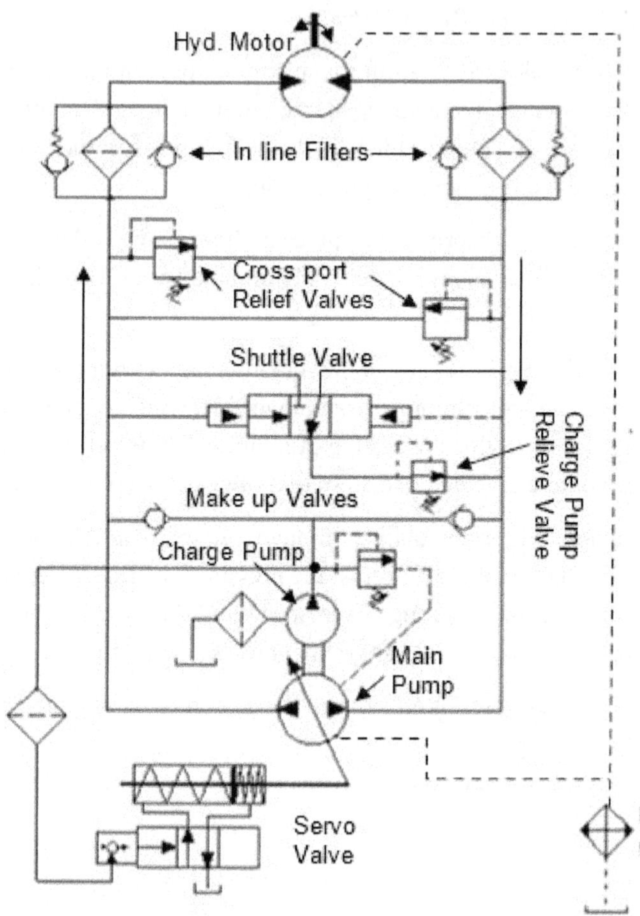

Figure 2.44 – Bi-direction Hydraulic Motor Control Circuit

On systems with hot oil shuttle valves, the tank port of the shuttle relief valve is sometimes ported into the hydraulic motor case drain line.

2.5.2 *Radial Piston Pump*

A radial piston pump has working pistons extend in a radial direction and symmetrically around the shaft. It is the main difference between the axial piston pump, which has axially rotating pistons. There are two variations of radial piston pumps:

1) A stationary-cylinder design uses springs to hold pistons against a cam that rotates with the main shaft of the pump

2) A rotating-cylinder design uses centrifugal force to hold pistons against a reaction ring

The radial piston pump comprises of a series of pistons radially installed in a cylindrical block around a rotor hub or is in a circular pattern of piston-cylinder arrangements. Pistons move in a radial direction with respect to the drive shaft.

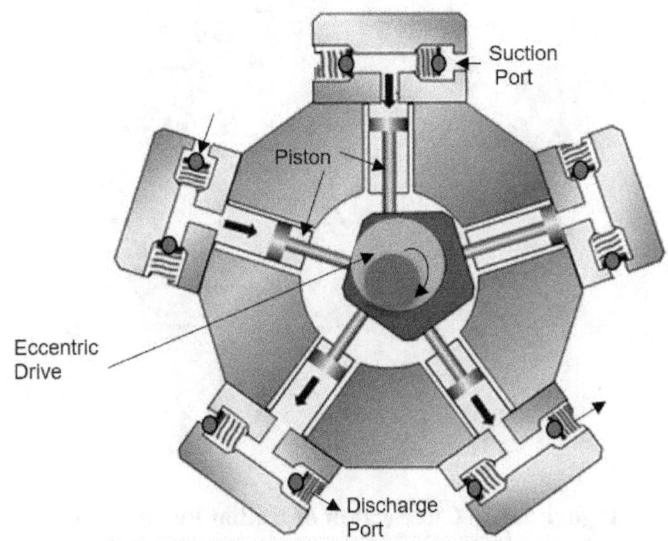

Figure 2.45 - Stationary-Cylinder Radial Piston Pump

The stroke of each piston is caused by an eccentric drive shaft or an external eccentric ring. The rotor, mounted eccentrically in the pump housing, forces the pistons in and out of cylinders as it rotates, which cause hydraulic fluid to be sucked into the cylinder cavity and then be discharged from it.

Inlets and outlets for the pump are in a valve in a central hub. Each piston is connected to the inlet port when it starts extending while it is connected to the outlet port when it starts retracting.

Each piston has spring-loaded inlet and outlet valves. As the inner cam rotates, fluid is transferred relatively smoothly from the inlet port to the outlet port.

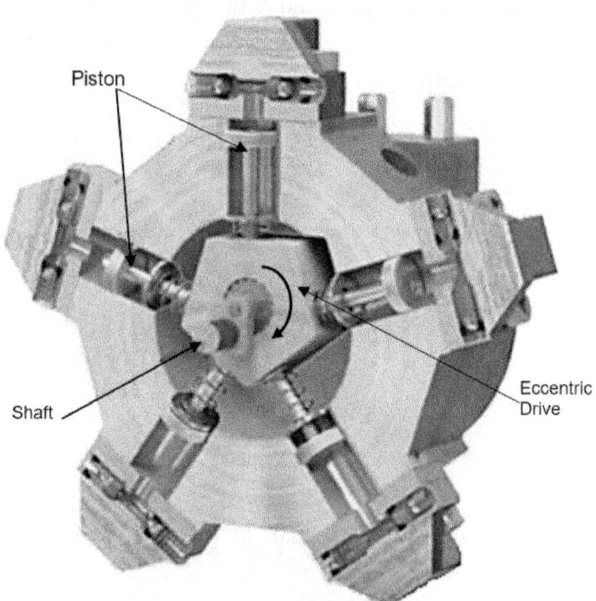

Figure 2.46 - Cut Section of Radial Piston Pump

2.5.2.1   *Rotating-Cylinder Radial Piston Pump*

The rotating-cylinder radial piston pump uses the same principle, but stationary cam and a rotating cylinder block as shown in Figure 2.47. This arrangement does not require multiple inlet and outlet valves and is consequently simpler and more reliable.

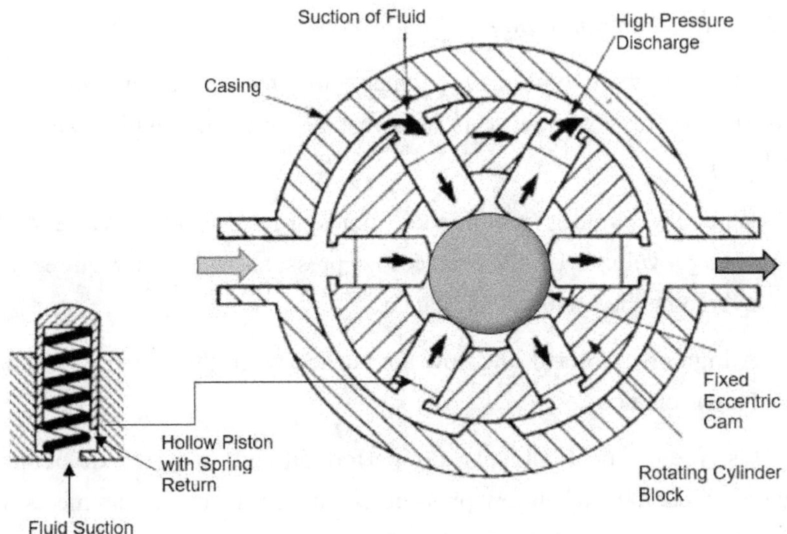

Figure 2.47 - Rotating-Cylinder Radial Piston Pump

2.5.2.2   *Advantages of a Radial Piston Pump*

✓ High efficiency

✓ High discharge pressure up to 1000 bar

✓ Low flow and pressure ripple due to the small dead volume in the workspace of the pumping piston

✓ Low noise level

✓ Very high load at the lowest speed due to the hydro-statically balanced parts.

✓ No axial internal forces at the drive shaft bearing

✓ High reliability

2.5.3 Combination Pump

There are the two basic requirements for any hydraulically powered system, where a workpiece is held in place by a hydraulic clamping cylinder.

a) When the cylinder / motor load extends or retracts, there is a need of a large volume of fluid at a low pressure which is required to overcome the frictional resistance.

b) A high pressure and low flow are needed when the cylinder / motor load is clamped.

This type of operation is usually performed with two separate pumps driven by load dependent low-pressure and high-pressure requirements in a hydraulic system are provided by two separate motors or a common electrical motor drive with two separate pumps where pump P1 is a high-pressure low-volume pump and pump 2 is a high-volume low- pressure pump as shown in Figure 2.49.

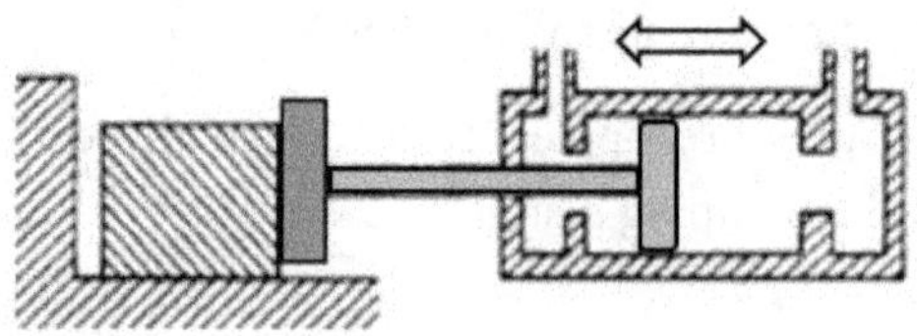

Figure 2.48   Hydraulic Clamping Cylinder

This type of operation is usually performed with two separate pumps driven by a common electric motor as shown in Figure 2.49. Pump P1 is a high-pressure low volume pump, while pump P2 is a high-volume low-pressure pump. Two relief valves are associated RV1 & RV 2 and a one-way check valve CV1 which allows flow from left to right, but blocks flow in the reverse direction.

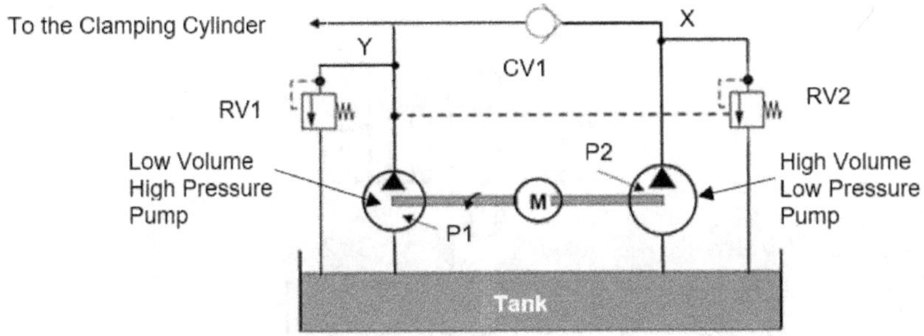

Figure 2.49 - Combination Pump in a Hydraulic System

The pressure relief valve RV1 is operated by high pressure. The pressure relief valve RV2 is remotely operated by the pressure at point Y but not operated by the pressure at point X.

Both relief valves are closed in low pressure mode and both pumps P1 and P2 deliver fluid to the load, but the majority comes from the pump P2 as its capacity is higher.

When the load is clamped, the pressure at A rises and relief valve RV2 opens. It results in all the fluid from pump P1 returning straight to the tank directly and the pressure at A to fall to a low value. The check valve CV1 allows the low-pressure high flow fluid from pump P2 consequently pressure at A rises to the level set by relief valve RV1.

This kind of arrangement saves energy as the large volume of fluid from pump P2 is returned to the tank at a very low pressure, and only a small volume of fluid from pump P1 is returned at a high pressure.

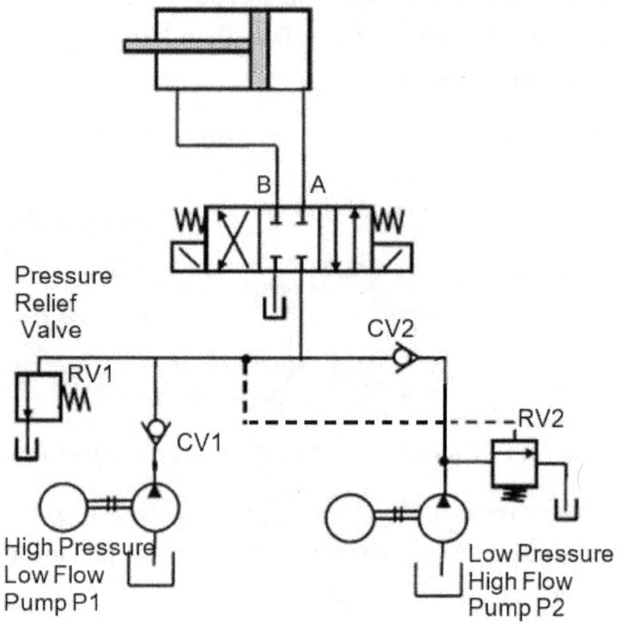

Figure 2.50

Combination Pump Circuit in a Hydraulic System

2.5.4 Warning Signs that Lead to Hydraulic Pump Failure

Some of the signs that indicate the danger of hydraulic pump breakdown are as follows:

a) Slow in Response

A slow response in hydraulic system means a loss of flow, which typically means internal leakage.

b) High Temperature

If the hydraulic system is exceeding the recommended temperature level of 82° C, due to a buildup of debris in the filters preventing the system from dissipating heat

c) Noisy System

If the hydraulic system is experiencing any aeration or cavitation, there's a good chance that the system will make very loud banging or knocking sounds, which will lead to pump failure.

2.5.5 Causes for the Failure of Hydraulic Pumps

2.5.5.1 Foreign Bodies or Mixtures

The major cause of hydraulic pump failure is due to contamination (by foreign bodies) of the hydraulic fluid. The clearances, ports and cavities of hydraulic pumps and valves are designed to carry hydraulic fluid; any water, debris, metal burs, dust, sludge, etc., will damage the system if they remain in the piping and rest of the system.

2.5.5.2 *Overheating*

Overheating in a hydraulic system can result in serious operational issues. Heat, we know has the uncanny ability to destroy seals, degrade the composition and change the viscosity of the hydraulic fluid, expand joints, and finally have a detrimental effect on the entire system.

2.5.5.3 *Over-pressure*

Hydraulic pump systems are quite sensitive. Wear and tear and system degradation is accelerated by the failure of joints, pipes, glands, seals, the pump itself and sometimes the system that it is driving too.

2.5.5.4 *Cavitation*

Cavitation is the formation of low-pressure vapour cavities; it occurs due to a fall in the absolute pressure *below the vapour pressure of the fluid.* The cavities can be quite small liquid-free zones like "bubbles" or "voids" formed due to partial vaporization of the fluid. Cavitation occurs when hydraulic fluid doesn't fully take up the space in the pump because of unusually high fluid viscosity, a very long intake line or a pump that is operating at abnormally high speeds.

When the cavitation bubbles collapse, they force energetic liquid into very small volumes, thereby creating spots of high temperature and emitting shock waves, the latter of which are a source of noise, damage to metallic components and piping.

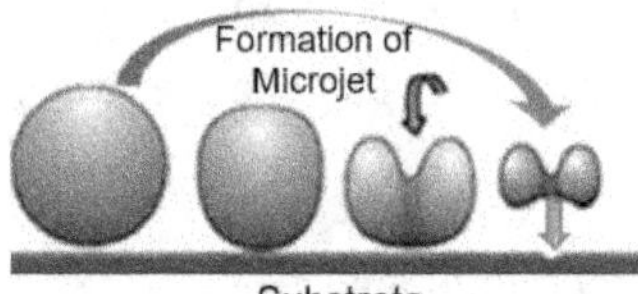

Although the collapse of a small cavity is a relatively low-energy event, highly localized collapses can erode metals, such as steel, over time.

The pitting caused by the collapse of cavities produces great wear on components and can dramatically shorten a pump's lifetime.

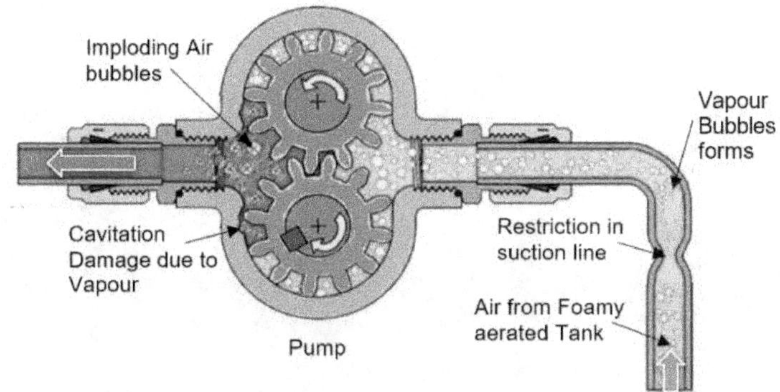

Figure 2.51   Formation of Cavitation in Hydraulic Pump

2.5.5.5 Aeration

Aeration is sometimes known as pseudo cavitation because air enters the pump's suction cavity. However, the causes of aeration are entirely different than that of cavitation. While cavitation pulls air out of the oil, aeration is the result of outside air *entering the pump's suction line*. Air in the hydraulic fluid can create problems when it is pressurised by the pump. When this happens, it can implode and dislodge debris, causing contamination and raising the temperature inside the pump.

It is important to understand that aeration and cavitation are not the same thing, but a relationship exists between them. Aeration simply refers to a presence of air in a liquid.

Vaporous cavitation is not related to aeration. Again, the bubbles created by this process are simply a liquid-to-vapour phase change - they do not contain any air.

Gaseous cavitation bubbles, however, may contain air.

***

⚓ Chapter 3 ⚓
Hydraulic Power Pack

3.1 The Need for a Hydraulic Power Pack

A hydraulic system will require a fluid power supply unit, a fluid storage and conditioning system which supply the hydraulic fluid into a system; it should also maintain the fluid at a suitable temperature and cleanliness level. A hydraulic power supply unit should also remove any air bubbles which may often enter the system and occurs through aeration.

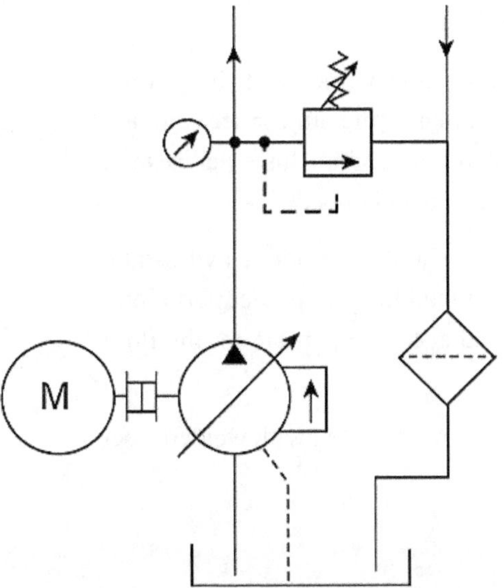

Figure 3.1 - A Hydraulic Power Unit

Bubbles can for example be drawn out of the solution by low pressures generally created because of high flow restrictions, which is like, but far more common than cavitation.

Power units should have alarm systems for problems in the main circuit such as loss of fluid or the low level of a reservoir tank or for high or low temperatures. The steering hydraulic system is one such example on board a ship.

3.2   Hydraulic Power Pack Components

3.2.1   *Reservoir*

An important component of a hydraulic system is the reservoir which holds the system's hydraulic fluid.

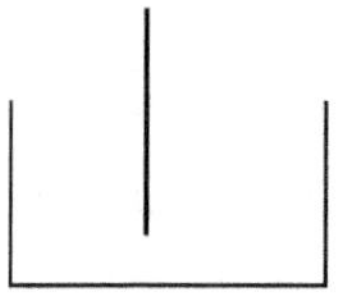

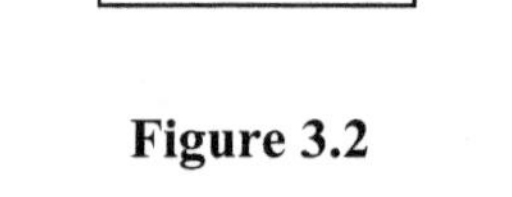

All hydraulic reservoirs used in marine application are open to the atmosphere and are known as vented reservoirs. This equalises the pressure both inside and outside.

Figure 3.2

Symbol of a Reservoir

The reservoir should provide a hydrostatic pressure head to feed the pump inlet port along with an air breather to compensate for the fluid that leaves it.

Reservoirs are constructed with welded steel plates.

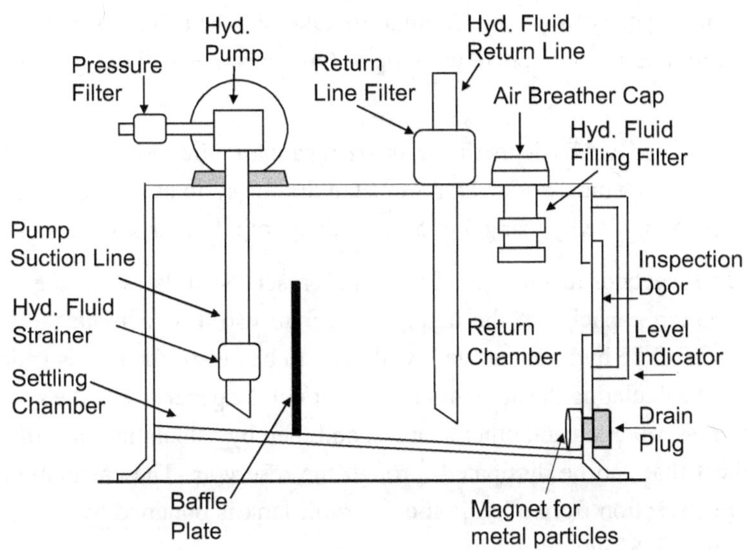

Figure 3.3 - A Hydraulic System Power Pack

The inside surfaces are painted with a sealer, to prevent the formation of rust which might in turn occur due to the presence of condensed moisture. It is common for the reservoir to have baffle plates and a shape suitable for allowing the dirt and air bubbles to settle out and leave the fluid as it passes through. The bottom plate is sloping and contains a drain plug at its lowest point, to allow complete draining of the tank when required. In order to access all the internals for maintenance, removable covers are provided.

3.2.1.1 *Capacity of the Reservoir*

The reservoir should be designed to allow the fluid to settle in the tank and re-circulate enough for optimal operation and for keeping the fluid clean by passing enough flow through the filters.

The capacity must be enough to take the actuators' drain down volumes and accommodate working volume changes without getting too low.

There are two basic methods for sizing a hydraulic reservoir. The first method which may work well for most hydraulic systems is by calculating the reservoir size by using 3 to 5 times the pump discharge rate.

The second method of sizing the reservoir relates to the heat dissipation capacity of the tank. In order to use this method, the heat balance of the hydraulic system will need to be determined. This is done by first calculating the amount of heat that will be generated in the system via pressure drops and other sources, and then by calculating the amount of heat that can be dissipated through the reservoir. The calculation of heat convection from a hydraulic reservoir tank is obtained by using the formula (in SI units):

Heat rejected P (kW) $= \Delta T \times A \times h \div 1000$

Where:

ΔT is the temperature difference between the oil and air, °C

A is surface area of the tank, excluding the base, m^2

h is the convective heat transfer coefficient for air, Watts $\div m^2$ (°C)

The value for h can be taken to be 12 for a normally ventilated space, 24 for forced ventilation, or 6 for poor air circulation. If the heat balance method is used, it is recommended that the reservoir be mounted above the ground to help ensure adequate air flow across the bottom and all four sides of the tank. For thermal expansion of the fluid and providing a free fluid surface for de-aeration, it is recommended that an air space be provided within the tank and above the oil level that is approximately 10% of the reservoir's fluid capacity.

3.2.1.2   Functions of a Reservoir

3.2.1.2.1   Stores Hydraulic System Oil

The level of hydraulic oil will vary during the operation of the system. As an example, the pump will have to supply more oil to extend a cylinder than to retract one. The reservoir in this case must have enough the capacity to hold the draining of the oil when the hydraulic system shuts down.

Sight level gauges show the volume of the fluid in the reservoir and are good early indicators of problems or leakage. Some level gauges have isolator valves built into them. These are useful because the glass is a potential failure point and so isolating the display will ensure you can continue working, even if the glass gets broken.

Level switches provide remote, visual or electrical warnings of low fluid levels and can also have a pump cut-out with very low fluid level, or warning at high fluid levels.

3.2.1.2.2   Cools the Oil

The reservoir is rectangular in shape to have maximum surface area so that the heat radiates to the atmosphere from its outer surface. One of the critical conditioning requirements of hydraulic fluid is that it is maintained at an optimal operating temperature.

The viscosity of the fluid increases as oil temperature drops, making it more difficult to pump, creating higher pressure drop and increasing the chances of cavitation.

The viscosity of the fluid decreases as oil temperature increases, which reduces lubricity, increases oxidation rate and can cause the contamination of fluid.

Figure 8.4 - A Hydraulic Reservoir

with a Heat exchanger and Accumulator

3.2.1.2.3   Purges Air from the System

As already mentioned, air bubbles are being drawn out of the solution by low pressures that are generally created because of high flow restrictions. Air in the hydraulic oil causes many problems and are mentioned below:

1) Oil oxidation as oxygen reacts with oil resulting in premature degradation.

2) Varnish formation as a result of the oil ageing.

3) Cavitation by the formation and collapse of gaseous oil cavities. It causes a decrease in pump efficiency and subsequent damage to pumps.

4) Noise and increase of temperature result in dynamic operating problems and system stiffness reduction.

5) Micro-diesel-effect.

6) Change in viscosity.

Note:

Aeration occurs when air contaminates the hydraulic fluid. Symptoms include foaming of the fluid, erratic actuator movements, and a banging or knocking noise when it compresses and decompresses as it circulates through the system.

Cavitation occurs when the pressure acting in a fluid is below the saturation pressure of a dissolved gas in the fluid. This causes the absolute pressure in that part of the circuit to fall below the vapor pressure of the hydraulic fluid, which results in the formation of vapor cavities within the fluid.

When these cavities encounter a region of higher pressure, they will collapse. Depending on the load pressure of the hydraulic pump, this can cause broad, high frequency vibrations, noise, material damage and degradation of the oil thereby leading to mechanical failure of the system components.

3.2.1.2.4 Allows Contaminants to Settle

Contaminants that the oil has picked up during the flow in the circuit will settle down to the bottom of the reservoir and form a sludge.

Periodically, the sludge must be cleaned up so that it does not enter the suction line of the pump. Build-up of thick sludge can cause temperature issues as it absorbs heat.

3.2.1.3   Components of the Hydraulic Reservoir

3.2.1.3.1   Air Breather

Air breather caps are required to compensate for the fluid volume changes e.g., for providing a stable pressure above the fluid head. Air entering the reservoir must pass through a filter that is as fine or finer than the main system filters to prevent ingress of dirt.

If any air has breached the system, it will rise to the top of the oil and will exit the reservoir through the breather cap. The breather cap should be checked and cleaned periodically and replaced annually whether it appears to be bad or not.

In extreme cases, such as aeration of the pump due to an air leak in the suction line or pump shaft seal, foaming of the oil will develop which may be more than the breather can handle.

Figure 3.5 - An Air Breather Cap with a Filter

3.2.1.3.2   Heat Exchanger

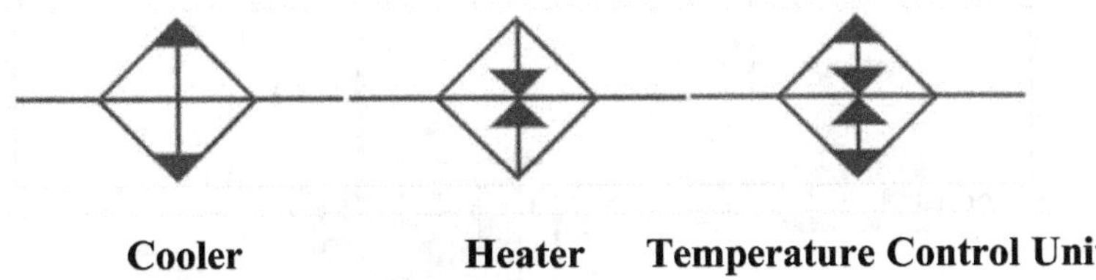

Cooler   **Heater**   **Temperature Control Unit**

Figure 3.6 – Symbols

A critical conditioning requirement of any hydraulic fluid is that it must be maintained at the optimum operating temperature. If the oil temperature drops, the viscosity of the fluid will increase and it will be more difficult to pump; this results in a higher pressure drop and also there is a chance of cavitation. As the temperature increases, the viscosity of the fluid decreases, resulting in reduced lubricity and increased oxidation rate.

To control the oil temperature, hydraulic systems use heat exchangers so that the fluid temperature can be within an optimal range and therefore viscosity, where the fluid has the best combination of properties useful to the components of the hydraulic system.

A low power hydraulic system can maintain the temperature of oil within its ideal temperature range by radiating the heat from the outer surface of the reservoir.

If the cooling effect from the reservoir is insufficient, a heat exchanger (or cooler) must be fitted to increase the heat dissipation rate. There are basically two types:

1) Air-cooled heat exchangers.

2) Water-cooled heat exchangers.

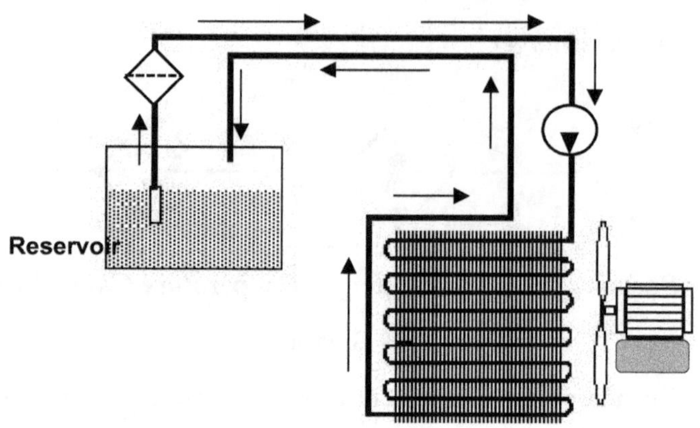

Figure 3.7 - Offline Cooling System of a Hydraulic System

When the heat to be removed is comparatively less, an air-cooled heat exchanger can be used. When the heat to be removed is higher, or its surrounding atmosphere is liable to be very hot, a water-cooled heat exchanger should be used.

3.2.1.3.3   Temperature Switch

Temperature warning and cut-out switches can be provided to ensure that the system does not work outside its design limit.

3.2.1.3.4   Immersion Heaters

Fluid immersion heaters often have built-in thermostats to ensure that the fluid stays above its minimum working temperature. This may be required before starting the pumps.

Figure 3.8 - Water Cooling of a Hydraulic System's Tank Access Cover

Hydraulic reservoirs require an access cover to be fitted on the side of the reservoir for cleaning and maintenance purposes.

3.2.1.3.5 *Baffle Plate*

One of the components in the reservoir for the settling of dirt and contaminants and reducing the turbulence of fluid before entering pump inlet is the baffle plate. Reservoir baffle / diffuser plates partition the return and supply lines thus allowing dirt and air to settle before reuse. This is done to prevent the same fluid from circulating continuously within the tank. In this way it is ensured that all the fluid is uniformly used by the system.

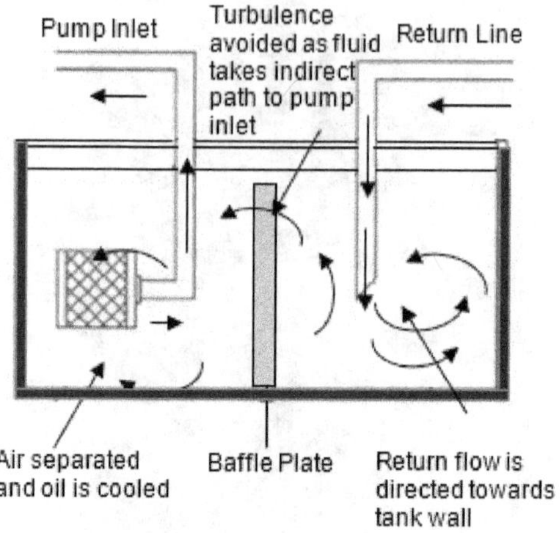

Figure 3.9 - Baffle Plate in a Hydraulic Reservoir

3.2.2 Filters

Hydraulic oil should create a lubricating film to keep precision parts separated. To reduce wear, this film should be thick enough to completely fill the clearance between moving parts. The actual thickness of a lubricating film depends on fluid viscosity, applied load, and the relative speed of the two surfaces.

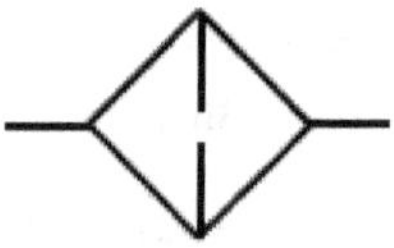

**Figure 3.10
Symbol of a Filter**

If the contamination particle is larger than the clearance between the surfaces, the result is that friction interference is increased and damage results. This damage introduces more contaminant particles. Therefore, the contaminant size should be kept smaller than the clearance and the number of these particles must be reduced as much as possible.

A hydraulic power system cannot be complete without the use of a filter as it keeps free from the hydraulic fluid, the contamination which contributes to 75% of premature failure in fluid-power systems. By keeping contaminants in check, it also helps to ensure that components and hydraulic systems perform as intended and last a longer time, with minimal unscheduled downtime. Contamination of the hydraulic fluid is caused by:

a) Initial contamination during commissioning by metal chips, foundry sand, dust, welding beads, scale, paint, dirt, sealing materials and contaminated hydraulic fluid.

b) Dirt contamination during operation owing to wear, ingress via seals and tank ventilation, while filling-up or changing the hydraulic fluid, exchanging components and replacing hoses.

3.3   Types of Contamination

Fluid can become contaminated due to multiple reasons like use and wear of the components and contamination brought in with new fluid or new components. Contamination in hydraulic systems can be classified into particle contaminants like metal particles from wear, dirt ingress or chemical contaminants such as water, air, heat, etc.

Particulate contaminants that circulate in fluid power systems lead to surface degradation like abrasion, erosion, and surface fatigue. This wear causes an increasing number of particles an accelerates failure.

If this chain reaction is not adequately controlled by reducing the contamination, early system failure occurs - like operating efficiency of the pumps, cylinder inner surfaces are damaged, and gaps grow larger leading to excessive oil leakage increases due to mechanical wear.

Examples of damage from contamination are accelerated component wear as mentioned, orifice blockage, formation of rust or other oxidation, depletion of additives, formation of other chemicals and oil quality degradation. Dirt causes trouble in a hydraulic system because it interferes with the fluid which has four basic functions:

1) To act as a medium for energy transmission

2) To lubricate internal moving parts of hydraulic components

3) To act as a heat transfer medium

4) To seal clearances between close fitting moving parts

3.3.1   Dirt in Hydraulic Fluid

Dirt interferes with the transmission of energy by plugging small orifices in hydraulic components like pressure valves and flow control valves. In this condition pressure has a difficult time passing to the other side of the spool. The valve's action is not only unpredictable and non-productive, but unsafe. The viscosity, friction, and changing direction, hydraulic fluid generates heat during system operation. When the fluid returns to the reservoir, it dissipates the heat to the reservoir walls. Dirt particles interfere with liquid cooling by forming a sludge which makes heat transfer to reservoir walls difficult.

It is evident that dirty systems run hotter than clean systems. The greatest problem with dirt in a hydraulic system is that it interferes with lubrication. Dirt can be divided into three sizes with respect to a particular component's clearances:

1) Dirt which is smaller than a clearance.
2) Dirt which is the same size.
3) Dirt which is larger than a clearance.

Extremely fine dirt, which is smaller than a component's clearances, can collect in these clearances - especially if there are excessive amounts and the valve or unit is not operated frequently.

This obstructs the lubricative flow through the passage. An accumulation of extremely fine dirt particles in a hydraulic system is known as silting.

Dirt which is about the same size as a clearance rubs against moving parts breaking down a fluid's lubricative film. Large dirt particles can also interfere with the lubrication by accumulating at the entrance and blocking the fluid flow between moving parts.

A lack of lubrication results in excessive wear, slower response, erratic operation, burning out of solenoids and accelerated component failure.

As a hydraulic equipment runs, it will generate contamination. This includes very fine metal particles that look like dust. These particles result from metal-to-metal contact especially during a component's break-in period because they have been recently machined and assembled together.

Over time, the size of the particles may get bigger, such as a chip from the surface of a ball bearing or a small piece that breaks loose from a gear tooth. Generated contamination could also include particles of rubber or polymer seals that wear out.

Generated contamination will affect the efficiency and productivity of hydraulic components. Every bit of generated contamination is likely to produce even more contamination in a dangerous domino effect. This type of contamination is unavoidable but can be kept under control by the proper use of filters.

3.3.2 *Water Contamination*

The most common chemical contaminant in hydraulic systems is water. The presence of water in hydraulic oil can have wide-ranging effects on system components because of its effect on the physical and chemical properties of hydraulic oil.

Rust in tanks, reduced lubrication characteristics resulting in accelerated metal surface wear are some of the most obvious physical results of excessive water, however the effects could be as diverse as the jamming of components due to ice crystals at low temperatures.

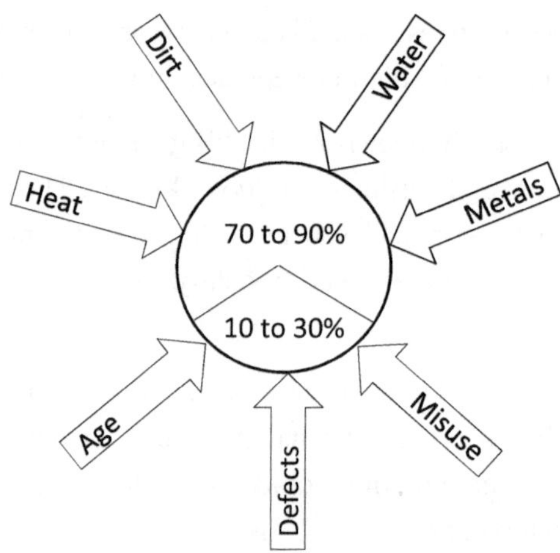

Figure 3.11 – Causes of Wear and Failure

3.3.3 *Chemical Contamination*

Chemical effects include additive depletion or deposition, oxidation, unwanted reactions which can result in the formation of acids, alcohols or sludges.

Oil becomes cloudy when it is contaminated with water above its saturation level. The saturation level is the amount of water that can dissolve in the oil's molecular chemistry and is typically 200 to 300 ppm at 20°C for mineral hydraulic oil.

Hydraulic oil containing just 0.1% water by volume usually reduces bearing life in half, while 1% reduces bearing life by 75%.

3.3.4 Air

Air in a hydraulic system can exist in either a dissolved or entrained (undissolved, or free) state. Dissolved air may not pose a problem, providing it stays in solution. When a liquid contains undissolved air, problems can occur as it passes through system components. There can be pressure changes that compress the air and produce a large amount of heat in small air bubbles.

This compressibility of air means that control of the system is lost. Air bubbles and frothing in the oil reservoir can cause major damage to pumps or it can also cause oil to "boil" out of the tank.

3.3.5 Heat

Excessive heat in hydraulic systems can also result in additive depletion or chemical changes to the oil.

3.4 Common Sources of Contamination in Hydraulic Systems

In general, there are four main sources of contamination in hydraulic oil.

3.4.1 Internally Generated Contaminate

Particles removed from the interior surface of the components will circulate in the system until they are removed. Each impact of one of these particles with a surface causes more damage.

This phenomenon is known as the wear regeneration cycle. Included in this is contamination from the catastrophic failure of components within the system.

3.4.2   Native Contamination

These are contaminant particles that were left in the system or any of its components during manufacture or repair and include contaminants such as welding slag, machining swarf, pieces of Teflon tape or excessive sealant.

3.4.3   Ingressed Contamination

This contaminate may enter with air flowing into the reservoir through the breather cap. Water will build up in the oil of a system operating in humid conditions if there is no protection against this built in to the reservoir.

3.4.4   Contaminated New Oil

New oil may not be clean enough for the system and is generally not clean enough for a modern, high pressure hydraulic system. The manufacturing process and the subsequent handling and storage introduce contaminants.

Another common source is dirt particles riding in on a cylinder rod. No rod seal can totally prevent the entrance of particles. This can be a major source of contamination on earth moving equipment operating in extreme conditions.

Furthermore, whenever the system is opened in any way such as when a hose is disconnected or fluid is topped up, there is the potential for contamination to ingress.

3.4.5 ISO 4406:2017

It is a method for coding the level of contamination by solid particles in hydraulic oil and provides a framework for reporting the concentration of contamination particles in hydraulic oil using an automatic particle counter.

3.5 Filters

3.5.1 Filter Types

1. Suction line filter – about 100 to 200 microns.

2. Pressure line filter – about 5 to 10 microns.

3. Return line filter – about 20 to 40 microns.

4. Off line filtration.

5. Full flow filters.

6. Proportional flow filters.

7. Filters with ΔP indicators and / or inbuilt bypass valves.

Figure 3.12 - Filters

3.5.2 *Filter Ratings*

Filters are rated in microns, which refers to the minimum particle size that the filter is designed to screen out.

Particles in the range of approximately 5 to 15 microns can cause problems in high-performing, high-pressure hydraulic systems which are much smaller than a human hair - about 90 microns in diameter, and likely not to be visible to the naked eye.

Another key metric for a filter is the Beta Ratio, which refers to the efficiency in which a given filter element removes particles of a given size. It is calculated using the ISO multi-pass test standard 16889:1999.

The importance of regular checks and cleaning / renewal of line filters cannot be overstressed. While replacing filter elements, it should be ensured that the new element is of the correct type and size.

3.5.2.1 *Beta (β) Ratio*

The Beta ratio is a measure of the filtration efficiency of a filter element; it is also the effectiveness of a filter to remove particles of a certain size or larger.

It can be determined by monitoring the fluid contamination levels upstream and downstream of the test filter. It is the ratio of the number of particles larger than a specified size which enters a filter compared to the number of the same size particles which go through without being caught.

Beta (β) Ratio = (Particle count in the upstream oil) ÷ (Particle count in the downstream oil)

3.5.3 *Filter Efficiency*

The filter efficiency is derived from the Beta ratio, and both convey the same information. It is given by:

Efficiency = $\frac{(\beta-1)}{\beta} \times 100$

A higher beta ratio points to the higher particle capture efficiency. For example, if 10,000 five-micron particles were measured, on average, before the filter, and 100 five-micron particles were measured after the filter, the beta ratio was 100.

Figure 3.13 – Filter Efficiency

3.5.4 Working Principle of a Filter

A filtration unit, such as a strainer or a filter, basically consists of a filter element that is encased in a housing and a filter head which together must be compatible with the fluid medium.

The filter housing protects the filter element. A filter can be designed to pass the entire flow through its filter element in each cycle as in a full flow filter or to pass only a portion of the flow in each cycle as in a proportional flow filter. It also includes necessary seals and ports. The filter element captures the contaminants in the fluid stream that passes through it.

Hydraulic fluid enters the filter assembly through the inlet port in the body and flows around the filter element inside the filter bowl.

Filtering takes place as the fluid passes through the filter element and into the hollow core, leaving dirt and impurities deposited on the outside of the filter medium.

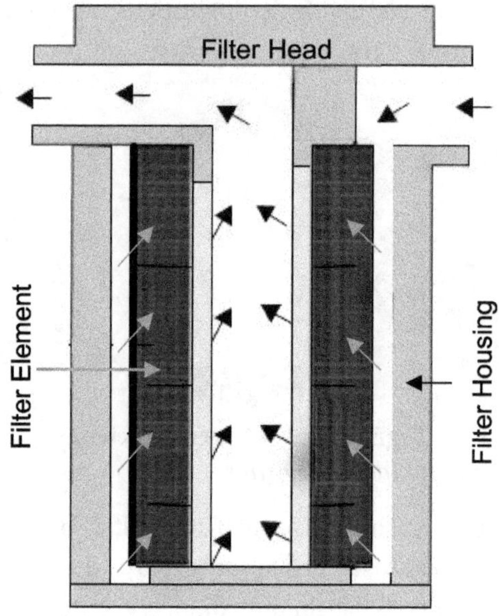

Figure 3.14

Construction of a Hydraulic Oil Filter

The filtered fluid then flows from the hollow core through the outlet port and continues through the system. Screen filters are constructed with many small, tightly woven wires which create a mesh or screen. These filters can be manufactured to a precise pore size and trap a pre-determined size of particles. An example of a screen filter would be the suction strainer on reservoir pump outlets. Suction strainers have a relatively coarse mesh designed to filter out coarser contaminants.

A full-flow micron-sized bypass filter is shown in Figure 3.15. This filter provides a positive filtering action; however, it resists flow, particularly when the element becomes dirty. A full-flow filter usually contains a bypass valve which automatically opens to allow the fluid to bypass the element when the flow of fluid is restricted because of contamination build-up on the element. Some filters have a mechanical indicator which also moves upwards to indicate that the filter is choked. There are a several types of filters, including the bag, screen and magnetic types.

The bag filter consists of a cloth bag through which the hydraulic fluid is pushed. The contaminants (being solid), are unable to flow through the bag as well. This is particularly useful in the filtering of dirt, rust, and particles introduced into the system by a cylinder rod.

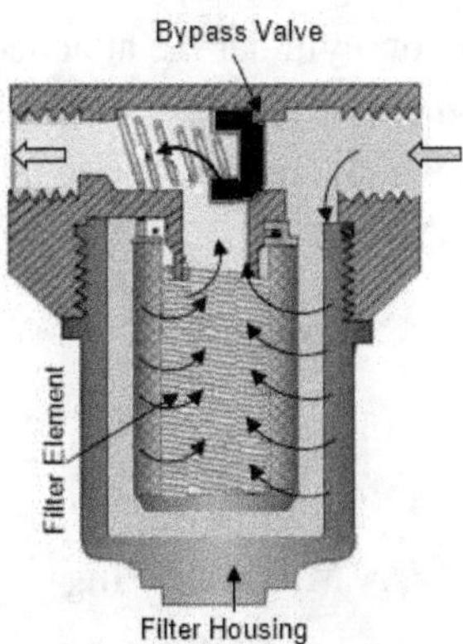

Figure 3.15 - Full-flow Type of Hydraulic Filter with a Bypass Valve

3.5.5 *Magnetic Filters*

The basic principle of magnetic filtration is that fluid flows around a magnetic rod or core which attracts ferrous particles, removing them from the fluid and ensuring that clean fluids are returned to the system.

Magnetic filters use magnetically charged plates that will attract any metallic contaminants.

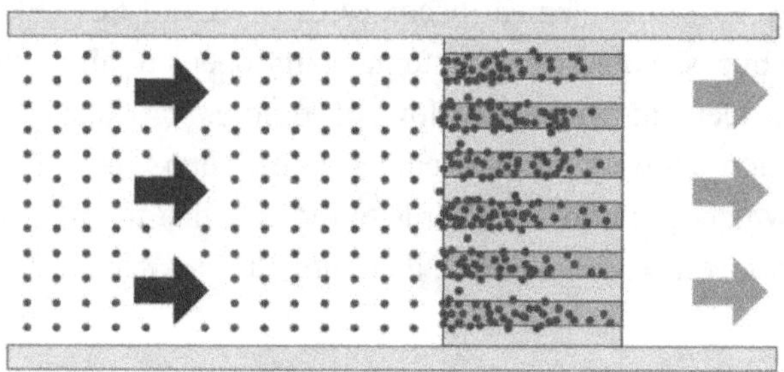

Figure 3.16 - Filtration by Magnetic Filter

3.5.5 *Magnetic Plug*

The most basic type of magnetic filter is a drain plug, where a magnet in the shape of a disc or cylinder is attached to its inside surface. Periodically, the magnetic plug is removed and inspected for ferromagnetic particles, which are then wiped away from the plug.

Figure 3.17
A Magnetic Plug

3.5.6 Strainers

Strainers are used to remove large solids from the water or oil supply. A strainer is constructed of a fine wire mesh screen, coarse filter or of screening consisting of a specially processed wire of varying thickness wrapped around metal frames.

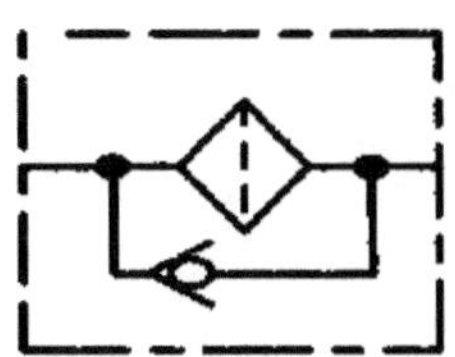

**Figure 3.18
Symbol of a Strainer**

It does not provide as fine a screening action as filters do, but offers less resistance to flow and is used in pump suction lines where pressure drop must be kept to a minimum.

It may have a check valve bypass so that in case the filter element is blocked, hydraulic oil can still flow.

3.5.7 Suction Filter

This filter is located on a suction port of the pump or is submerged in the reservoir and attached to the suction line leading to the pump. A fine filter on a pump suction side would require the filter to be very large which will handle the flow and have an extremely low-pressure drop.

3.5.8 Pressure Filter

A pressure filter typically $(10 - 20\ \mu)$ is designed to withstand peak system pressure and is generally installed between the pump outlet and the rest of the components. It will reduce the chance of contamination from pump generated contamination reaching the components downstream.

Figure 3.19 - A Suction Filter

Filters often include a bypass valve with a cracking pressure of about one bar (14.5 psi) to protect the filter from collapsing or bursting and do not get damaged during a cold start or near their end of life.

3.5.9 Contamination Indicator

A wide range of clogging indicators including an alarm system are available to show when the filter elements need replacement.

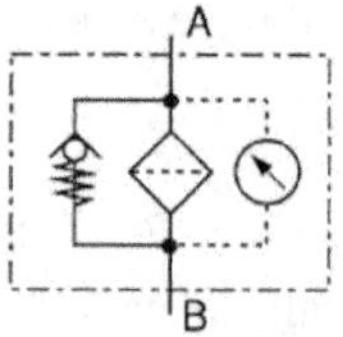

Figure 3.20 - A Contamination Indicator

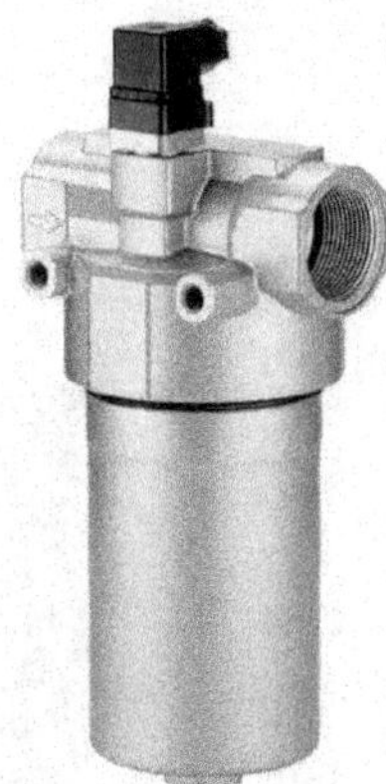

Figure 3.21 - A Pressure Line Filter

The effectiveness of the filter can be checked by a contamination indicator which is controlled by the drop in pressure. The pressure ahead of the filter rises as the contamination increases which can act on a spring-loaded piston. As the pressure increases, the piston is pushed against the spring and the piston movement is visible or else it is converted into an electrical or optical indicator by electrical contacts.

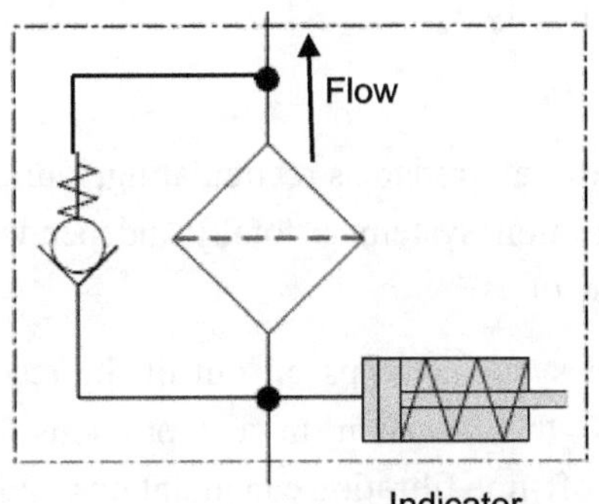

Figure 3.22 – A Piston-type Indicator

3.5.10 *Return Line Filter*

Return filters may be installed either in-line or inside the reservoir and are used to remove any contamination that has entered the system via cylinder rods, etc.

As low-pressure filters cost less than high-pressure filters, they are often used as the main cleaning workhorse in the system with the finest filtration rating.

Low-pressure return line filters also have bypass and visual or electrical clogging indicator options that warn when elements need changing.

Figure 2.23 - Return Line Filter

3.5.11 *Off-line Filters*

Off line filters are referred to as recirculating, kidney loop or auxiliary filtration. This filtration system is totally independent of a machine's main hydraulic system.

An independent system pumps oil out of the reservoir, through the filter, and back to the reservoir in a continuous fashion. With this "polishing" effect, off-line filtration can maintain a fluid at a constant low contamination level.

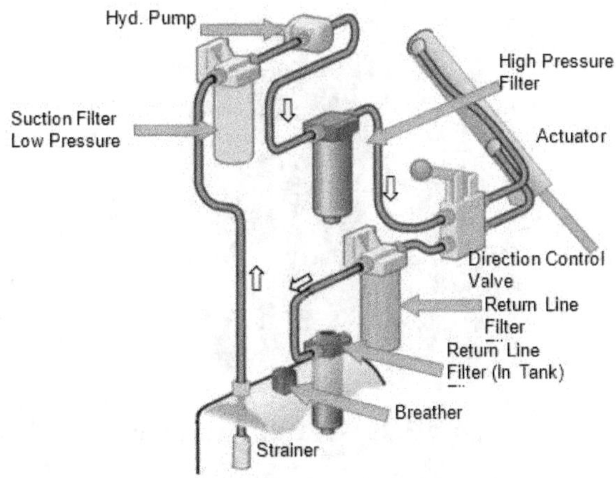

Figure 3.24 - A Hydraulic System with Filters

3.5.12   *Duplex High-Pressure Filter*

When a single filter assembly is applied, the system must be shut down or bypassed whenever the filter element requires servicing. If such a condition is undesirable (in a power plant, for instance) then it would be prudent to install a duplex filter.

A duplex type features at least two filter housings with a transfer valve separating the housings. The flow can be routed through one housing or both depending on the valve.

When one of the filters is fully loaded, the operator switches the valve to activate the standby filter and then services the dirty filter. The duplex filter avoids the shutting down of a system during a filter change.

Figure 3.25 – A Duplex Filter

3.6   Auxiliary Components of a Hydraulic Power Pack

3.6.1   Suction Line

The pump inlet line is a large diameter, short pipe that draws fluid from the reservoir into the pump. Its size is critical for ensuring a low fluid velocity and therefore as positive a head as possible at the pump. Often flexible pipes are used to isolate pump vibration from the tank.3.6.

3.6.2   Pressure Hose

A short flexible hose is commonly used between the pump and is the first component in the circuit. This helps to reduce noise and vibration and allow the pumps to operate on their mounts.

3.6.3   Pressure Test Point and Gauges

For safety and maintenance, a pressure gauge and/or test points are recommended. These allow operators to quickly check the condition of the power unit and are vital during commissioning and maintenance.

3.6.4 Relief Valve

Relief valves are essential to protect the system against over pressurisation and potentially dangerous failures. They may also be used to unload the system for pump start-up or standby modes.

3.6.5 Isolation Ball Valve

An isolation ball valve will help protect personnel during maintenance and stop the fluid from syphoning out of the reservoir when items are changed or removed. These valves are often lockable so that people cannot open them and pressurise the system when the maintenance engineer has closed them for maintenance.

3.6.6 Filling Point

Filling points should be used to pump new fluid into the reservoir and through the return line filter to ensure it is as clean as possible.

These can be a simple inline filter located after the return filters or may be part of a separate fluid conditioning circuit that takes fluid out of the reservoir before pumping it back in clean and at the correct temperature.

3.6.7 Drain Plug

The bottom part of the reservoir is usually provided with a downward gradient and a drain plug at its lowest point so that the system fluid can be drained completely without any difficulty.

3.6.8 Diffusers

It is used in combination with a return-line filter to slow down the return fluid. The reduced velocity prevents foaming and re-suspension of deposited dirt. It also reduces turbulence and noise.

3.6.9   Tank (Reservoir) and Magnetic Tank Cleaners

The reservoir is rectangular in shape to have maximum surface area so that the heat radiates to the atmosphere from its outer surface. One of the critical conditioning requirements of hydraulic fluid is that it is maintained at an optimal operating temperature.

Tank cleaners with permanent magnets can be used for attracting and holding the abrasive ferrous particles.

3.6.10   Conclusion

Modern high-pressure hydraulic systems with components built to closer tolerances are susceptible to many types of contamination. We are aware by now that contaminants can cause the premature wear of internal surfaces. They also promote leakage and clog the flow paths.

Therefore, an efficient and correctly sized filtration system should be an integral part of every hydraulic system to separate the particulate matter of a specified size or greater from the system fluid. They should be fitted at appropriate locations in the hydraulic circuit for the effective control of contamination.

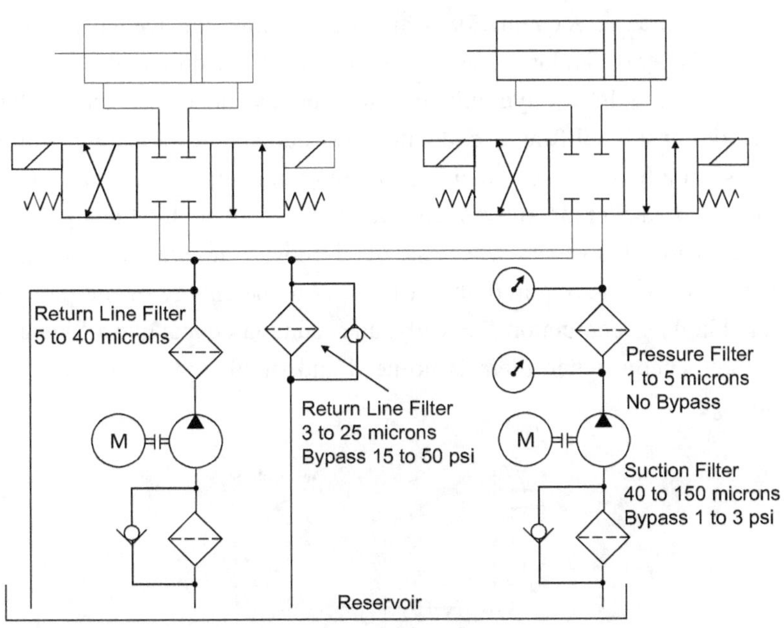

Figure 3.26 - Various Type of Filters used in a Hydraulic System

3.7   Hydraulic Accumulator

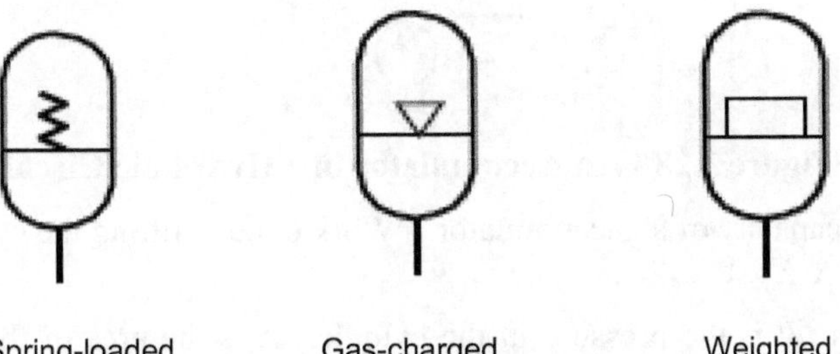

Figure 3.27 – Accumulator Symbols

The hydraulic accumulator is an energy storage device which stores potential energy and is released on demand to force oil into the circuit at a later stage to drive a hydraulic machine for any sudden and intermittent operation just like lifting a load with a hydraulic crane, etc. For example, in case of a hydraulic crane, a large amount of energy is needed to lift a load when the crane moves up, which is supplied by the hydraulic accumulator. However, when the load moves downwards, no large external energy is required at that time; now the energy of the pump is stored in the accumulator. Basically, an accumulator acts like a flywheel. It stores energy when there is no need and supplies it when there is a shortage.

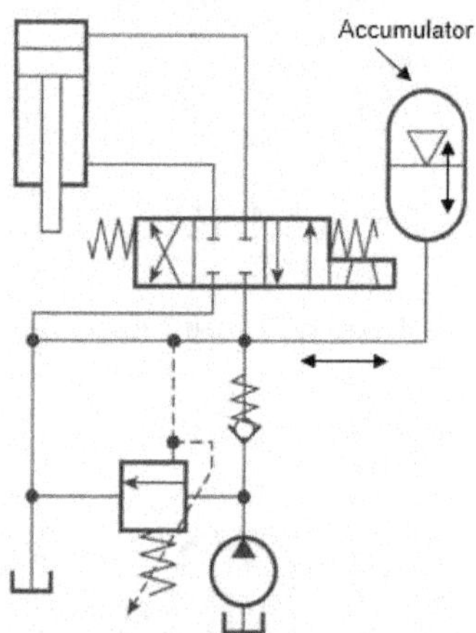

Figure 3.28 - An Accumulator in a Hydraulic Circuit

The capacity of an accumulator = Work done in lifting the cylinder / ram = P x A x L

Where P is the pressure in the cylinder, A is the area of the sliding cylinder and L is the length of the stroke.

Most accumulators are energized with inert gas, such as nitrogen while some have dry air, and the symbol shows a partition separating the top and bottom of the oval. Hydraulic fluid, pressurized by a hydraulic pump, forces the piston of the accumulator to compress the gas in the chamber.

The compressed gas or air can store the energy just like a spring or flywheel. When the hydraulic system needs the extra flow, the compression energy will be released to compensate for the system's needs.

3.7.1   Functions of the Hydraulic Accumulator

3.7.1.1   Provides transient flow in a short time

The hydraulic accumulator can provide a peak flow in a short time in an intermittently working hydraulic system. The hydraulic accumulator can help in decreasing the size and reducing the weight of the hydraulic system.

3.7.1.2   Compensates for the leakage and maintains the pressure

The accumulator can provide the flow and maintain a constant pressure for the actuation unit that does not move for a long time but needs to maintain constant pressure.

3.7.1.3   Works as an emergency power supply

When the hydraulic power supply system suddenly stops feeding the hydraulic fluid, the hydraulic accumulator can provide the fluid to keep the system operational in case of an emergency.

3.7.1.4   Absorbs the pressure ripple of the hydraulic system

As the hydraulic system has an inherent flow ripple and fluid-solid coupling vibration, its pressure ripple will influence the actuation system's performance. The accumulator can absorb the pressure ripple and maintain the pulsation within an allowable range.

3.7.1.5   Absorbs the impact pressure

When the control valve suddenly changes the direction or the actuation system suddenly stops, the accumulator can absorb their impact pressure.

A hydraulic accumulator is divided into three parts namely:

1) Air chamber (for air or compressed gas)
2) Piston
3) Oil chamber (hydraulic fluid)

Accumulators use compressed gas to apply force to a hydraulic fluid. Identical in their operating principle, piston, bladder and diaphragm accumulators use different mechanisms to separate the gas from the fluid.

3.7.2   Bladder Accumulators

Bladder accumulators feature a flexible rubber bladder that is non-pleated and housed within a steel shell. One end of the bladder has a valve stem fitted with a gas valve.

A poppet valve, normally held open by a spring, prevents the bladder from being extruded out of the hydraulic port during shutdown.

The units suit most applications, are dirt- tolerant, respond quickly and work well with water and low-lubricity fluids.

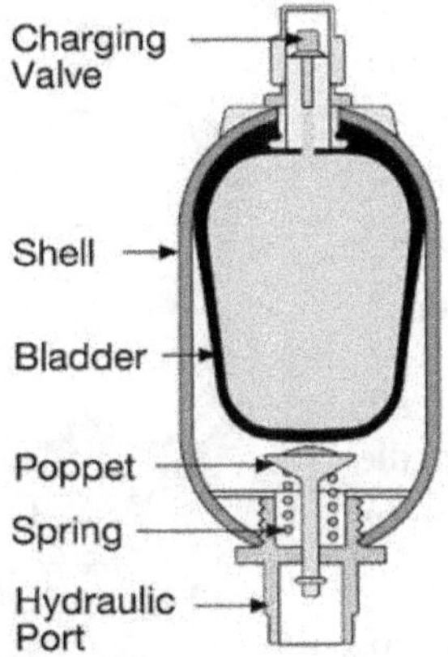

Figure 3.29 - A Bladder Accumulator

3.7.3 *Diaphragm Accumulators*

Diaphragm accumulators operate much like bladder accumulators. The difference is that instead of a rubber bladder, it uses a one-piece moulded elastic diaphragm that is mechanically sealed to a high-strength metal shell.

The flexible diaphragm separates gas and fluid and a button moulded to the bottom of the diaphragm prevents it from extruding out of the hydraulic port.

A diaphragm accumulator can handle higher compression ratios of up to 8 to 10:1 because the rubber barrier does not distort to the same degree as a bladder.

These units are compact and lightweight, simple, inexpensive, dirt tolerant, and respond quickly.

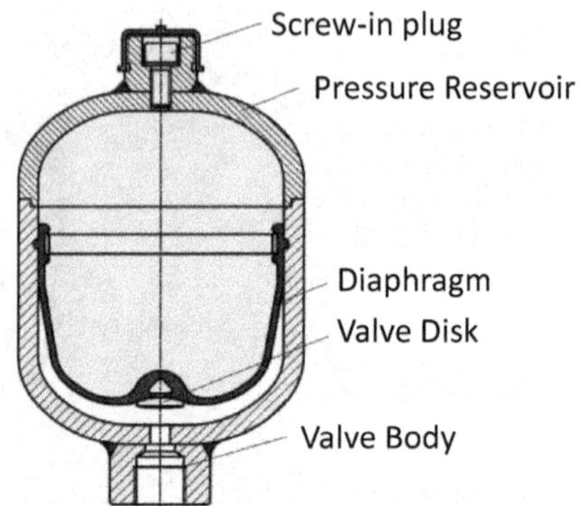

Figure 3.30 - A Diaphragm Accumulator

3.7.4 *Piston Accumulators*

Piston accumulators are much like hydraulic cylinders but without a rod. They consist of a fluid section and a gas section, with the movable piston separating the two with a charging valve at the gas end, and a hydraulic cap at the fluid end.

The advantages include high flow rates, a wide temperature range, high compression ratios, and the ability to withstand external forces.

Piston units work well with auxiliary gas bottles. Piston accumulators are generally recommended for large, stored volumes.

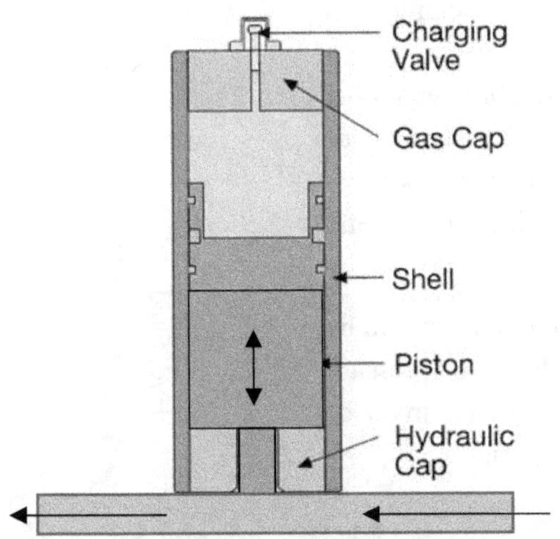

Figure 3.31 – A Piston Accumulator

3.7.5 *Metal Bellows Accumulators*

Metal bellows accumulators are used where a fast response time is not critical, yet reliability is important. Emergency brake accumulators are a good application for metal bellows accumulators.

The metal-bellow accumulators consist of a pressure vessel with a metal bellows assembly separating fluid and nitrogen. The accumulator is like a piston accumulator, except a metal bellows replaces piston and piston seals.

Metal bellows accumulators will be slow in responding to pressure changes due to increased mass of the piston and bellows.

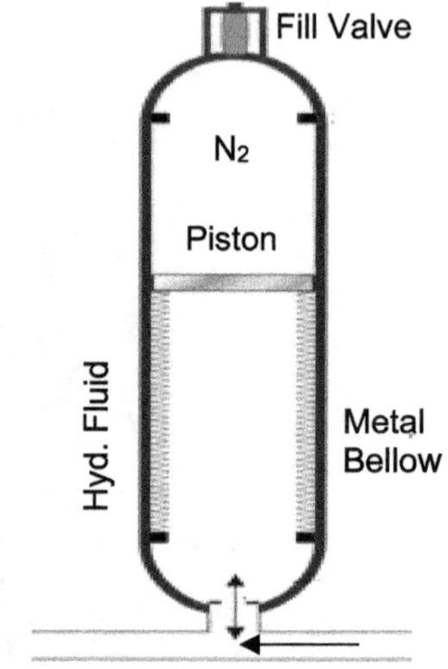

Figure 3.32 – Metal-Bellow Accumulator

***

For Books on following Subjects

- Business, Management & Finance
- Career Development, Career Guides
- Catering & Hotel Management / Recipes
- Civil Engineering
- Computers
- Communication
- Dental / Health / Medical
- Economics
- Electrical Engineering
- Electronics & Communication
- English
- Entrepreneurship
- Environmental Engineering
- Event Management
- Fiction
- Forensic Science
- General Titles
- HRD
- International Trade
- Law
- Learning Disability
- Mathematics
- Mechanical Engineering
- Media
- Mobile Computing
- Motivation & Self Help
- Parenting
- Patent
- Physics
- Project Management / Software Engineering
- Real Estate
- Statistics

Publishers We Represent

www.ingramcontent.com/pod-product-compliance
Lightning Source LLC
LaVergne TN
LVHW021710210726
843510LV00015B/1227